Praise for *Tell Me Everything*

"No matter what profession you are in, knowing how to get people to cooperate and share information with you is a skill few master. This is the best book I've read on how to achieve that—filled with practical insights and backed by decades of real-world experience."

—Joe Navarro, former FBI Agent and Author, *What Every Body Is Saying*

"As social creatures, humans constantly seek to obtain information from others. *Tell Me Everything* shows readers how to create settings that increase your influence on others, as well as how to know when the truth has really come out. Integrating behavioral science, neuroscience, and decades of experience, this book is a must-read for anyone who talks to others—that is, everyone!"

—Paul J. Zak, PhD, Author, *The Little Book of Happiness*

"As someone who's built my career on forging unbreakable trust in high-stakes environments, I recognize Brad Beeler's expertise as the gold standard—honed not in academia but through 25 years as a US Secret Service Agent and elite polygraph examiner, extracting truths in intense, high-profile cases. Leaders, sellers, negotiators, or anyone seeking deeper connections: grab this book to transform your interactions."

—Robin Dreeke, former Chief of the FBI Counterintelligence Behavioral Analysis Program and Bestselling Author, *It's Not All About Me*, *The Code of Trust*, and *Sizing People Up*

"Built on decades of experience and grounded in behavioral science, this book teaches the skills that matter most: how to build trust, get honest answers, and influence with integrity. It makes complex psychology easy to understand and apply, without losing its depth or scientific accuracy."

—Dr. Abbie Maroño, Behavioral Scientist, Author, *The Upper Hand*

"Very few books manage to blend heart, science, and actionable skill the way *Tell Me Everything* does. Brad Beeler doesn't just teach you how to spot deception or build trust; he teaches you how to do it ethically, humanely, and with purpose. This book is a masterclass in connection, forged in the trenches of the most difficult cases imaginable. If you lead, protect, parent, investigate, or influence, you'll walk away better equipped to understand people, and more importantly, to make them feel understood."

—Christopher Hadnagy, Founder, Social-Engineer, LLC and The Innocent Lives Foundation, and Author, *Human Hacking*

Tell Me Everything

Tell Me Everything

A Secret Service Agent's Proven Strategies for Earning Trust, Revealing the Truth, and Communicating with Anyone

Brad Beeler

Matt Holt Books
An Imprint of BenBella Books, Inc.
Dallas, TX

This book is designed to provide accurate and authoritative information about personal and professional development. Neither the author nor the publisher is engaged in rendering legal, accounting, or other professional services by publishing this book. If any such assistance is required, the services of qualified professionals should be sought. The author and publisher will not be responsible for any liability, loss, or risk incurred as a result of the use and application of any information contained in this book.

Matt Holt is an imprint of BenBella Books, Inc.
8080 N. Central Expressway
Suite 1700
Dallas, TX 75206
benbellabooks.com
Send feedback to feedback@benbellabooks.com

BenBella and *Matt Holt* are federally registered trademarks.

Printed in the United States of America
10 9 8 7 6 5 4 3 2 1

Library of Congress Control Number: 2025036183
ISBN 978-1-63774-842-8 (hardcover)
ISBN 978-1-63774-843-5 (electronic)

Editing by Katie Dickman
Copyediting by Michael Fedison
Proofreading by Jenny Bridges and Rebecca Maines
Text design and composition by PerfecType
Cover design by Brigid Pearson
Printed by Versa Press

CONTENTS

PART III

Strategic Communication & Influence

Timing, Mindset, Influence, and Listening

PART IV

Detecting Deception and Uncovering Truth

How to Spot Lies, and Elicit the Truth

INTRODUCTION

This book is a comprehensive blueprint for mastering influence, connection, and communication—distilled from decades of real-world experience in the most demanding environments imaginable. If you've ever struggled to get the truth from someone, persuade a difficult colleague, close a deal, or connect with a distant teenager, the tools in this book will revolutionize how you engage with others.

As a retired Secret Service Special Agent, I spent 25 years navigating high-stakes conversations with hardened criminals, vulnerable victims, and some of the most powerful people in the world. I've observed world leaders engage in tense negotiations, studied what makes people open up—or shut down—and developed a series of communication strategies that increase the likelihood of getting honest answers and real commitments.

Throughout my career, I conducted more criminal polygraph examinations than any other Special Agent in Secret Service history—not because it was required, but because it allowed my partners and me to give back to the local law enforcement agencies that supported our protective and investigative missions. We used the polygraph and our interview skills to assist them with their most difficult cases, often involving murder or child exploitation.

I've trained top interrogators, law enforcement officers, and intelligence professionals from agencies like the FBI, CIA, NSA, and local police departments around the world. I've tested what works—and discarded what doesn't.

But this book isn't about high-profile interrogations or law enforcement tactics. It's about human interaction—how to read people, build trust, influence conversations, and uncover the truth in any situation. The skills I've refined over decades—detecting deception, using influence strategically, and understanding what's said (and unsaid)—are just as applicable in parenting, sales, leadership, negotiations, and everyday interactions.

HOW THIS BOOK WILL CHANGE THE WAY YOU COMMUNICATE

You don't have to be an interrogator or a government agent to benefit from the principles in this book. If you interact with people, these strategies will give you the edge in every conversation.

Parents will learn how to recognize when their child is holding something back, create the kind of trust that invites honesty, and ask clear, purposeful questions that go beyond the usual short answers—like "I'm fine."

Sales professionals will develop the ability to read clients more accurately, uncover unspoken objections, and guide them toward a "yes" without pressure or manipulation.

Leaders and managers will master how to inspire trust and get their teams to communicate openly—even in high-stakes situations.

Negotiators will discover how to use strategic silence, body language, and timing to gain the upper hand—whether closing a business deal or negotiating a raise.

Anyone looking to improve their communication skills will learn how to make an unforgettable first impression, detect hidden emotions, and turn every conversation into an opportunity for influence and connection.

Because when people feel like they can tell you anything, they will tell you everything.

WHAT YOU'LL LEARN IN THIS BOOK

Every chapter is packed with actionable techniques and real-life stories to elevate your communication skills. You'll discover how to:

Make First Impressions Count. Use body language, vocal tone, and subtle cues to establish instant trust and authority.

Engage All Your Senses in Communication. Learn to harness all five senses for more impactful and effective interactions.

Master the Science of Timing and Setting. Recognize the ideal moments and environments that encourage people to open up.

Harness the Power of Ethical Influence. Use proven psychological techniques to foster trust, drive action, and steer conversations toward positive outcomes.

Spot the Lie. Develop the skills to identify deception using scientifically proven methods and techniques honed through decades of real-world experience.

Encourage Truthful Disclosure. Once deception is recognized, you will learn a systematic approach to ethically guide someone toward admitting the truth—without pressure, confrontation, or manipulation.

The book is organized to reflect the natural flow of human interaction, addressing how to make a strong first impression, facilitate disclosure, and navigate critical moments when truth—or deception—arises.

WHY BRAZILIAN JIU-JITSU MADE ME A BETTER COMMUNICATOR

Throughout my law enforcement career, I was exposed to some of the most mentally and emotionally taxing cases imaginable—many involving crimes so heinous they weighed on me long after I left the interrogation room. Over time, I needed an outlet—something to help me decompress from these encounters. That's when I discovered Brazilian Jiu-Jitsu (BJJ), a martial art focused on ground fighting, submissions, and using leverage and technique to control an opponent—regardless of their size or strength.

What began as a method to manage stress quickly evolved into a guiding philosophy. I soon recognized the same traits that led to success on the mats also extended to conversations, negotiations, and interrogations. My instructor, Professor Guybson Sa, emphasizes several core principles that I believe are relevant to many areas of life, particularly communication:

"The mats don't lie." In BJJ, techniques that fail under pressure are discarded—only those that work in real-world scenarios survive. Communication is no different. The strategies in this book aren't just theories—they have been battle-tested in high-stakes interrogations, negotiations, and everyday conversations.

"Position leads to submission." In BJJ, you can't force a submission—you must first secure the right position. The same applies to communication. Before you can persuade, negotiate, or uncover the truth, you must establish trust, gain control of the conversation, and create the conditions for success. Just as a skilled fighter must read their opponent's movements and adapt in real time, an effective communicator must learn to read body language, adjust tone, and recognize the right moment to speak—or remain silent.

"Master what matters most." There are countless techniques to learn in BJJ, but most success in competition stems from mastering just a select few. Great instructors don't waste time trying to teach everything; they focus on what works. Repetition builds confidence, while precision delivers results.

That same mindset has shaped my entire approach to communication. You don't need to excel at everything—you need to be outstanding at what truly matters. A few high-impact skills, practiced deliberately and applied with intention, can make the difference between a forgettable conversation and one that creates real change.

These aren't just helpful tips; they are the core habits of elite communicators—skills that, when fully mastered, foster deeper trust and significantly increase your chances of productive outcomes in any conversation.

That's the purpose of this book: to help you identify those essential skills, train them with intention, and apply them when it counts. That's what enables you to stay calm under pressure, adapt in real time, and connect in ways others cannot.

Are you ready to unlock the full potential of your communication skills?

Let's begin.

PART I

The Foundations of Effective Communication

Mastering First Impressions and Preparation

CHAPTER 1

Horns and Halos

"You never get a second chance to
make a first impression."
—Will Rogers

The idea of "making a good first impression" is deeply rooted in science and profoundly impacts our social and professional lives. Forming an initial impression goes beyond mere social etiquette; it's akin to wearing a metaphorical halo or horns, representing how others perceive us based on early interactions. This rapid assessment process is rooted in our evolutionary history, where quick judgments were crucial for survival in potentially hazardous environments. Today, this same process continues to significantly impact professional opportunities and personal connections.

Despite the well-known importance of first impressions, many books fail to offer actionable tactics for improvement. The following chapters aim to bridge that gap by presenting practical strategies to apply immediately to make a solid and favorable first impression in any setting.

These strategies are not just based on abstract theories but have proven effective in real-world situations, empowering you to take control of your communication and feel more confident in your interactions.

A LESSON FROM THE FIELD

A vivid illustration of the "horns and halos" concept unfolded toward the end of my career during a criminal search warrant with my colleague Ryan, a fellow Secret Service Agent. As we cleared the house looking for potential threats, we entered the kitchen and found ourselves face-to-face with two dogs: a muscular pit bull and a tiny Chihuahua. Predictably, our attention focused on the pit bull, its imposing presence, and the breed's reputation, instantly earning it a set of metaphorical horns. As an animal lover, the last thing I wanted was to harm a family pet, so we focused on keeping the pit bull calm while unconsciously assigning a halo to the seemingly harmless Chihuahua.

Then, without warning, the Chihuahua made its move. It launched from behind, sinking its teeth into a very sensitive area between my legs. In that split second of shock, I questioned every decision that had led me to this moment. Fortunately, my tactical pants—crafted from fire hose–like material—saved me from what could have been a painful and embarrassing injury. To this day, Ryan relishes telling anyone who will listen how a 10-pound Chihuahua turned me into a chew toy, dangling from my groin and swinging back and forth like a deranged acrobat. At the same time, the pit bull watched the chaos unfold with what must have been a look of amusement.

That day, I learned a lesson I'll never forget: Appearances can be deceiving. Whether in human interactions or the animal kingdom, never judge a book by its cover.

THE EVOLUTION OF FIRST IMPRESSIONS

Imagine yourself as a prehistoric ancestor, moving cautiously through unfamiliar territory. A band of strangers appears on the horizon. Modern spoken language doesn't exist—you can't rely on words to gauge their intent. Survival depends entirely on instinct and observation. Your eyes first go to their hands—empty or armed? Then to their posture—open or tense? Their facial expressions, tone, and subtle movements are your only clues. Misread the situation, and it could cost your life. Correctly interpret it, and it could forge a new alliance. Our ancestors may have relied on first impressions for survival, but today, we rely on them for social and professional success. Science proves we still form these judgments in the blink of an eye, using the same ancient circuitry.

Research shows that people can assess a person's traits—such as trustworthiness, competence, likability, aggressiveness, and attractiveness—within just 100 milliseconds of seeing their face. In a study examining this phenomenon, participants were shown a series of faces for a fraction of a second and asked to evaluate them based on these traits. Even when given more time to analyze the faces, their initial impressions remained remarkably consistent.[1] This finding highlights how quickly and persistently first impressions are formed—faster than the blink of an eye—and how difficult they can be to change.

The ability to quickly assess facial cues is thought to have provided significant evolutionary advantages. This skill was crucial for our ancestors in swiftly identifying potential threats or allies in their environment, enabling immediate decisions about whom to approach or avoid. These snap judgments played a crucial role in survival and fostering social bonds. A warm, friendly expression acts like a halo, inviting trust, while harsh tones or closed-off body language create a horn effect, discouraging connection. Whether in ancient encounters or modern interactions, first impressions set the stage for every relationship that follows, influencing whether someone feels comfortable opening up or instinctively shuts down.

PHYSIOLOGICAL CONSIDERATIONS OF FIRST IMPRESSIONS

When engaging in conversations, it's essential to consider the physiological dynamics at play. Our brains are wired to make quick assessments, thanks to the limbic system and the amygdala—our "threat detection" centers. The limbic system is a complex set of structures in the brain that deals with emotions and memory. Among these structures, the amygdala plays a key role in processing emotions like fear and pleasure and is crucial in forming emotional memories. When it perceives a threat, the amygdala triggers a "fight or flight" response, preparing the body to confront or flee the danger. Navigating past this instinctual alarm system is crucial to gaining someone's trust and accessing their information.

The impact of first impressions extends beyond immediate interactions and shapes future perceptions and decisions. When someone creates a positive first impression, it builds a reservoir of credibility and trust that can be utilized to their advantage, often without your awareness. Conversely, if someone makes a negative first impression, it becomes incredibly challenging for them to change your perception, regardless of subsequent positive interactions. Think of this as making deposits into a trust bank, which others can draw upon to influence or manipulate you in the future. For instance, a colleague who initially impresses you can more easily sway your opinion, even if their subsequent contributions are not as substantial. This is because their positive first impression gives them a credibility cushion.[2]

On the other hand, a bad first impression creates a deficit in the "trust bank." Rebuilding trust and credibility from this point requires many positive interactions, making it lengthy and challenging. This is why changing a negative perception once it's formed is so hard. The evolutionary basis of "horns and halos," while beneficial for quick assessments, has drawbacks. Our initial judgments of "friend" or "foe" can be mistaken, yet humans tend to stick with these first impressions for consistency. This tendency leads to confirmation bias, where we favor information that supports our initial assessment, even if it's inaccurate.

THE DANGER OF CONFIRMATION BIAS

Confirmation bias is like wearing a pair of blinders that make us see only what supports our existing views. This is especially problematic when someone dangerous earns our trust through a strong first impression, or when a good person is dismissed because of a poor one.[3] This bias can lead to flawed decision-making and reinforce misconceptions.

In law enforcement, confirmation bias can profoundly shape the trajectory of an investigation. When detectives form a strong initial impression—believing a suspect is either guilty or innocent—they may unconsciously filter all subsequent evidence through that lens, potentially overlooking key details that contradict their assumptions. This is why it's essential to evaluate each piece of evidence objectively and remain open to revising initial judgments as new information emerges.

Remaining open-minded is essential—not only when evaluating evidence but also when assessing the behaviors and demeanor of the individuals involved. People under stress, fear, or emotional overwhelm may appear defensive, evasive, or inappropriate, leading to unfair assumptions. The case of Amanda Knox provides a well-known example: her behavior after her roommate's murder was widely viewed as inappropriate, fueling suspicion and contributing to a wrongful conviction that was later overturned.

Conversely, individuals who intend to deceive are often skilled at making a positive first impression, using charm or composure to mask their true intentions. Ted Bundy is a notorious example—he leveraged a disarming, trustworthy demeanor to lure victims who might otherwise have been more cautious.

Awareness of these dynamics is critical—not just in law enforcement but in parenting, leadership, and everyday decision-making. The ability to assess people and situations objectively—without being anchored by early judgments—is a powerful skill in any context. This is also why the way you present yourself to the world matters. Body language, attire, and demeanor shape conclusions before a single word is spoken.

I've encountered many situations where detectives, interviewers, or hiring managers became convinced of a person's guilt, innocence, or suitability based solely on first impressions. Yet my polygraph examinations and investigations often revealed the opposite, demonstrating just how misleading initial impressions can be. I teach this principle to encourage a more objective, nuanced approach to assessing people. However, as the following example illustrates, I'm not immune to the very cognitive traps I caution others to avoid.

I was contacted to assist in the investigation of a missing person / homicide case in which the police department had identified two suspects, both members of a motorcycle gang. One of the suspects was a certified "one-percenter." This term originated in the 1940s, claiming that 99% of motorcyclists were law-abiding citizens, and the remaining 1% were outlaws engaged in various criminal activities. This suspect wore a "1%" patch on his biker jacket to signify his affiliation with this outlaw subgroup. He was a large convicted felon with an almost dark aura surrounding him. He was what most people would visualize as the prototypical villain in a Hollywood action movie. The second suspect was a probationary member of the gang, extraordinarily timid and unassuming. Based on the initial facts of the case, I decided to polygraph the timid individual first. I designed the examination to determine if he had any involvement in the disappearance and possible death of the missing woman.

The subject failed the polygraph examination, prompting me to begin a follow-up interview. My preconceived notions influenced my approach. I assumed he knew about the disappearance and that the felon was the main culprit. Throughout the interview, I focused on the possibility that he had witnessed a violent act perpetrated by the felon and was covering up out of fear or allegiance. This continued for several hours, during which he repeatedly said, "That's not it." I interpreted these statements as objections and persisted with my original line of questioning based on my confirmation bias.

Fortunately, a local detective was observing from outside the interview room. My confirmation bias was laser-focused on viewing this suspect as merely a witness or accessory after the fact. I believed that obtaining his account of what he saw or heard could be used in a subsequent interview with the felon. During a break, one of the detectives asked to sit in on the interview. Shortly after resuming the interview, the detective interjected with a crucial request: "You keep saying that's not it. Well, just tell me what it is."

The suspect hesitated for a moment and then said, "I killed her; I cut her body into six pieces and dumped them into the river." He subsequently led us to the location where he had disposed of her body, and search teams found her remains. My confirmation bias had prevented me from viewing this individual as a cold-blooded killer. I am grateful this bias did not infect the clear-eyed detective. As a result of her actions in obtaining the suspect's confession, he was convicted of murder and sentenced to life in prison.

So, how do we counteract these biases and ensure we see the full picture? Here are some practical tips to avoid falling victim to confirmation bias:

- **Start with a Neutral Perspective:** Approach each new person without preconceived judgments. Avoid labeling them as a friend or foe until you've gathered enough information to form an accurate assessment.
- **Look Beyond Body Language:** While body language is an important clue, it can also be misleading. Nervousness doesn't always indicate guilt, and confidence doesn't necessarily mean honesty.
- **Pause Before Making Conclusions:** When you feel the urge to make a quick judgment, especially in high-stakes situations, take a moment to pause. This brief hesitation prevents you from relying too heavily on first impressions, allowing you to approach new information objectively.
- **Question Your Assumptions:** Just as you would scrutinize someone else's statements, critically examine your own beliefs. Regularly check if you're focusing on details that confirm your initial impression or overlooking evidence that challenges it.
- **Seek an Outside Perspective:** A fresh perspective from someone uninvolved in your assessment process can help reveal blind spots

and counter personal biases. Consider consulting someone who is not influenced by your initial impression in critical situations.

- **Separate Emotions from Analysis:** Notice if discomfort or suspicion affects your judgment. Stepping back emotionally allows you to assess facts and behavior more objectively, minimizing the risk of mistaking nervousness for guilt or confidence for truthfulness.

By staying open, questioning your assumptions, and welcoming diverse perspectives, you can approach each interaction with a balanced and investigative mindset, fostering more accurate and objective judgments.

Understanding the power of horns and halos is just the beginning. To truly connect with others and influence outcomes, we must master the deeper mechanics of communication itself—how our words, tone, and body language harmonize to create a lasting impact. Effective communication requires aligning sound, imagination, sight, and movement. Let's dive into the core components of communication—the *lyrics* (our words), the *soundtrack* (our tone), and the *dance* (our body language)—and explore how each of these components can be used to elevate the way we communicate.

CHAPTER 2

Lyrics, Soundtrack, and Dance

"Words mean more than what is set down on paper. It takes the human voice to infuse them with shades of deeper meaning."
—Maya Angelou

Communication is the currency of connection, shaping our careers, relationships, and overall success. Recent studies show 85% of job success comes from having well-developed soft and people skills, while only 15% comes from technical skills and knowledge.[1]

If Socrates or Shakespeare were dropped into today's digital era, they would marvel at our technological progress—but be puzzled by how our communication has, in many ways, regressed. Emojis and acronyms now serve as our modern-day cave paintings or hieroglyphics—brief, symbolic messages exchanged without the benefit of real-time feedback or the ability to see the recipient's reaction. Success lies in how well we can package our words, tone, and body language together in order to engage, inspire, and influence.

Let's break it down into its essential elements: the *lyrics* (the words we use), the *soundtrack* (the tone of our delivery), and the *dance* (our body language). Together, these components form a symphony—a performance that can either captivate or repel, depending on how it is orchestrated.

To illustrate this, I often tell a story from my journey, one that began when I was 16 and trying to connect with my best friend, Doug, who is deaf. At first, our conversations were challenging. I had to learn to enunciate clearly, convey emotions through body language, and tune in to his facial expressions to ensure we were understanding each other. Later, I took an American Sign Language course in college, which deepened our communication and friendship. Doug primarily relied on lip-reading, but I quickly realized that expressive gestures and body language were the backbone of our interactions—not my spoken words.

Imagine watching a horror movie without the soundtrack. You'd lose the ominous music that builds tension and signals impending danger. This was Doug's everyday experience: He couldn't rely on vocal tone, pitch, or volume shifts to gauge emotions. We had to communicate over the phone with a TTY machine, where Doug would type his message, and an operator would read it aloud to me. This was before emojis, so the operator would add inflection to convey Doug's tone, adding layers of emotion to his typed words. Yet even with these tools, Doug was missing paralinguistics—the subtle cues in how spoken words convey so much of what's left unsaid.

But Doug had adapted. Through years of observing people's faces and body language, he had developed an almost superhuman ability to detect hidden emotions. His insight taught me that communication is far more than spoken language. Watching professional sign language interpreters brings this home—you'll see their faces and bodies fully engaged, enhancing each sign and adding a richness of meaning.

My interactions with Doug highlighted the value of fully investing in a conversation. To have a meaningful exchange, I needed to be fully engaged, ensuring I spoke at a rate of speech and with the appropriate body language and facial expressions that assisted in making sure Doug understood. Also, when Doug verbalized his words or signed, I had to be completely engaged to ensure I didn't miss something—this level of commitment led to truly enriching conversations. Too often today, people engage in conversations like "ships passing in the night," listening only to respond rather than fully participating. Many conversations have become what I call "transactional talk"—a surface-level exchange without genuine involvement.

Now, let's examine the importance of holistically packaging words, vocal tonality, and body language to convey a message.

LYRICS: THE POWER OF WORDS

Words are arrangements of letters that convey meaning. The average American has an active vocabulary of between 25,000 and 30,000 words. We draw from this mental dictionary to construct sentences that make sense, allowing us to articulate thoughts, convey complex concepts, provide instructions, and share knowledge.

Certain situations require careful word choice. For instance, in my law enforcement role, I refer to a crime as a "situation" when speaking with a suspect. The word "crime" has long-term negative connotations, whereas "situation" implies something more manageable and fixable. Here are some other examples of word substitutions used to soften the impact:

- Theft—Taking of money
- Kill—Cause the death
- Burglary—Trespassing
- Murder—Took their life

Organizations have recognized the importance of carefully choosing their words in business. For example:

- Surgery—Procedure
- Shot—Injection
- Used—Pre-owned
- Problem—Challenge

Without language comprehension, communication hinges on tone and body language—the soundtrack and dance of interaction. This is evident in how we connect with babies and dogs. Unable to grasp the meaning of words, they rely entirely on the tone of our voice and the movements of our bodies to gauge our intentions. You could speak complete nonsense to a dog or a baby, but as long as your tone is calm and your body language is open, you'll likely be met with trust and warmth.

This phenomenon highlights a critical truth: While words matter, they often follow the lead of the tone that conveys them. Winston Churchill's speeches during World War II didn't stir a nation solely because of elegant phrasing—it was his calm defiance, deliberate pauses, and unwavering tone that rallied hearts.

The same sentence, spoken with a different inflection, can convey hope—or surrender. That's the power of tone—the soundtrack of our communication: It makes or breaks the message before the words finish landing.

SOUNDTRACK: THE IMPORTANCE OF PARALINGUISTICS

As discussed in the previous section, word choice is just one aspect of the communication equation. Paralinguistics is all the vocal elements, such as tone, pitch, volume, speed, and intonation. It also encompasses nonverbal cues like pauses, hesitations, and sighs. Understanding paralinguistics is crucial in communication as it adds an emotional layer to words, shaping how they are received.

The same sentence can convey different emotions depending on the tone used. For example, "I'm fine" can indicate well-being, sarcasm, or frustration based on the tone. My wife has approximately 127 different ways of saying, "I'm fine." Twenty-five years of marriage have given me a metaphorical decoder ring for deciphering these variations depending on the situation.

Research shows listeners often rely more on tone than words to interpret emotions.[2] Tone also enhances clarity and engagement. A lively and varied tone maintains interest, while a monotone delivery can lead to boredom. A classic example is the teacher in *Ferris Bueller's Day Off*, whose monotone voice lulls the entire class to sleep. Influential speakers use pitch, pace, and volume changes to emphasize key points and keep the audience engaged.[3]

My Brazilian Jiu-Jitsu instructor, Guybson Sa, grew up in Brazil speaking Portuguese. He loved the Red Hot Chili Peppers despite not understanding their lyrics. What resonated with him was the soundtrack and how it made him feel. The music videos he grew up watching of lead singer Anthony Kiedis, bass player Flea, and drummer Chad Smith performing created a connection. Similarly, some of the greatest songs have lyrics that make little sense, yet the soundtrack and dance make them memorable.

Just as the soundtrack shapes the emotional impact of our words, our body language—the *dance* of communication—reinforces or contradicts our message. While tone influences how words *sound*, body language determines how they *feel*. A confident stance, open gestures, and purposeful movement can amplify credibility, while crossed arms, fidgeting, or lack of eye contact can create doubt or disinterest. Communication isn't just about what we say or how we say it—it's also about how we *show* it.

DANCE: THE ROLE OF VISUAL PRESENTATION

Visual presentation, including body language, facial expressions, and gestures, often conveys emotions and attitudes more effectively than words alone. Studies demonstrate that facial expressions and gestures are paramount in expressing feelings.[4] Integrating visual presentation with words and tone creates a holistic communication experience. In political debates, visual presentation can significantly influence public perception.

During the 1960 US presidential debates, John F. Kennedy's confident tone and composed appearance contrasted sharply with Richard Nixon's less polished demeanor. Those who listened to the debate on the radio thought Nixon won, while television viewers believed Kennedy was the victor, highlighting the critical role of visual presentation.[5]

The rise and fall of the pop music phenomenon Milli Vanilli offers a fascinating look at the complex interplay between lyrics, soundtrack, and dance. I must sadly admit, as a freshman in high school, decked out in newly purchased parachute pants, I attended one of their concerts. While their lyrics might not have been considered poetic, their electrifying stage presence and undeniable charisma propelled them to stardom. The group, masterminded by producer Frank Farian, was built around performers with the right image and charm. Farian brought in two male models from Germany and France who were skilled dancers; however, rather than singing, they lip-synced to recordings made by different vocalists. When the truth emerged that Milli Vanilli had been a fabricated group, the actual singers put out an album of their own. Despite their authentic vocal abilities, they failed to duplicate the group's prior success, highlighting the significant impact of image and presentation on public perception.

This dynamic between appearance and talent is mirrored in popular talent shows. Programs like *The Voice* attempt to eliminate visual bias, focusing solely on vocal ability during the initial auditions. Singers perform for a panel of four celebrity judges who keep their backs turned to the stage, making decisions based purely on the quality and emotion of their voices. An impressed judge presses a button, causing their chair to turn around, allowing them to see the performer for the first time. This format ensures that judgments are made without influence from a singer's appearance, stage presence, or body language, emphasizing the auditory experience and showcasing how isolating a single sense can lead to a more focused and objective evaluation.

In contrast, *American Idol* employs a broader assessment approach. Judges evaluate contestants on multiple factors, including vocal ability, appearance, and stage presence. This comprehensive evaluation gives a more holistic view of a performer's potential. The success of *American Idol* in identifying mainstream talent demonstrates the value of enhancing all aspects of communication—words, tone, and body language.

PRO TIP—A THREE-STEP EXERCISE TO IMPROVE YOUR COMMUNICATION SKILLS

Want to fine-tune your communication skills? Try this simple yet powerful exercise I have used to train students for many years. It serves to assess and improve how you come across to others.

1. **Watch Yourself on Mute**—Record a short conversation, presentation, or interview. Play it back with the sound off and observe your body language, facial expressions, and gestures. Do you appear confident, engaged, and approachable? Or do you fidget, slouch, or look disinterested?
2. **Listen Without Watching**—Now, turn off the video and listen to the audio only. Pay attention to your tone, pace, volume, and inflection. Does your voice sound engaging and confident or monotone and unsure? Are there unnecessary pauses or filler words?
3. **Look for Key Moments of Disconnect**—Watch the full video with sound and visuals. Pause at key moments (especially when making important points) and ask: Is my body language reinforcing what I'm saying? Is my tone matching my message? Even brief moments of incongruence can erode trust. Identify any disconnects and adjust those elements in your future delivery. Practicing this regularly will refine your communication style and help you develop a more polished and effective presence in any conversation, meeting, or presentation.

Mastering communication isn't just about what we say—it's about how we say it, how we sound, and how we present ourselves. We create lasting impact by aligning our lyrics, soundtrack, and dance, ensuring our words resonate long after the conversation ends. Now let's shift our focus to enhancing the quality of our conversations. This begins with gathering background intelligence—understanding the person and subject matter—before the interaction occurs.

CHAPTER 3

Pre-Interview Intelligence

"Give me six hours to chop down a tree, and I will spend the first four sharpening the axe."
—Abraham Lincoln

Success in communication doesn't happen by chance—it happens by preparation. Whether you're leading a negotiation, conducting an interview, or building rapport with a stranger, understanding who you're speaking to before the conversation begins gives you a powerful advantage. Just as a pilot reviews a flight plan before takeoff, effective communicators don't enter high-stakes conversations unprepared. The more you know about the person and their context, the more you can anticipate responses, avoid friction, and guide the discussion toward a meaningful outcome. Researching a person's background, interests, and experiences doesn't just help you navigate potential challenges—it also helps fill natural lulls in conversation and establish genuine connections.

For example, job applicants should research the company and position before an interview to tailor their responses and show how they align with the organization's goals. Taking the time to understand the company's mission, values, and expectations enables candidates to speak confidently and demonstrate their knowledge, making a stronger impression.

When teaching communication and elicitation to students from the law enforcement or intelligence communities, I often compare effective communication to the streaming music platform Spotify. Think of effective communication like Spotify's music algorithm—the more it learns about you, the better it adapts to your preferences. Skilled communicators do the same: They start broadly, adjust based on feedback, and refine their approach in real time.

Just as social media platforms track likes, shares, and time spent on content to personalize user experiences, great communicators pay attention to verbal and nonverbal cues to tailor their message in real time. They don't bombard the listener with irrelevant information; instead, they present content in a way that holds attention and builds rapport.

OBSERVATIONS FROM SOMEONE'S SOCIAL MEDIA ACCOUNTS

By examining a person's likes, dislikes, friends, travels, and photos, we can gain valuable insights into their personality and behavior. This information reveals their social circle and potential addictions (good and bad), shedding light on their character. For example, reviewing social media posts has been instrumental in my elicitation efforts, providing a deeper understanding of the suspect's motivations and mindset.

By thoroughly understanding the subject we are about to discuss, we begin from a position of advantage. This knowledge allows me to steer the conversation in a way that is tailored to their interests, much like a metaphorical Facebook or Instagram reel filled with curated content that captivates their attention. Approaching a conversation with knowledge about the other person's interests, needs, and background demonstrates respect and understanding. This establishes trust, which is the cornerstone of influence.

In the past, people guarded their private thoughts in diaries and journals, locked away from prying eyes. Today, in our oversharing social media world, people voluntarily broadcast their interests, opinions, and daily lives for all to see. This shift has created an unprecedented opportunity: With just a little research, we can gain valuable insights before ever meeting someone.

For communicators, this is a gold mine. Social media, online history, and public data allow us to create a dossier on the person we're about to engage with, giving us a home-field advantage in conversation. A quick search can reveal:

Interests & Passions—Hobbies, sports teams, favorite books, or travel destinations.

Emotional Triggers—Complaints, frustrations, or causes they advocate for.

Recent Life Events—Moves, job changes, or celebrations that can serve as natural icebreakers.

By leveraging pre-interaction intelligence, we can tailor conversations to build rapport, avoid awkward silences, and foster a sense of familiarity. Whether preparing for an interview, negotiation, or casual meeting, this background knowledge increases our chances of a smooth and productive exchange.

Case Studies in Social Media Observations

Before interviewing a subject who was accused of child exploitation, I searched for her X/Twitter activity. Several tweets stood out. One focused on where she had recently moved from, and the others were regarding previous interactions with her friends. Upon greeting her, I commented about her accent and said I had an affinity for guessing where people were from. Of course, I guessed correctly based on prior knowledge from her X/Twitter account. This was a great icebreaker and lowered her anxiety in the initial stages of the interaction. Also, several of her previous tweets about being taken advantage of by others due to her forgiving nature were utilized. I told her later during the interaction that she had a very forgiving personality and that those around her took advantage of that trait. Her eyes lit up when I said this, and after some initial hesitancy after meeting me, she began to lower her guard. During the subsequent interaction, she confessed to numerous horrific crimes against children.

In another child exploitation case in Missouri, I delved into the suspect's social media accounts to gather information about his favorite sports teams, food preferences, and hobbies. This research provided valuable insights into potential talking points that could be instrumental in developing rapport and alleviating any anxiety the subject might experience during the interaction. Notably, I did not have to feign interest in these shared interests; the social media profiles served as cues guiding my focus.

One area of shared interest emerged as both the suspect and I had traveled to the same foreign country. This common ground became a focal point of our conversation, lasting 10–15 minutes. This shared experience, brought to light through prior research, allowed for a more natural and effective rapport-building process. Without background research, this shared interest might have remained undiscovered and rapport diminished.

In a chilling turn of events, the subject eventually admitted to engaging in the assault of several children. This case is a stark example of how leveraging insights from social media can facilitate rapport-building and uncover shared experiences that may play a crucial role in the investigative process.

In another case, a subject shared numerous pictures of his pet pit bull on social media, indicating that this pet was a significant part of his life. While I was gathering personal information, he talked about some negative experiences from his youth. During the subsequent interview, I used the concept of nurture to influence the outcome. I explained to him that pit bulls are among the most misunderstood animals. He agreed with this idea. I continued by saying that a pit bull that is well cared for and loved makes a wonderful pet. However, a pit bull that is abused, like a mistreated human, is likely to have a different trajectory in life and behave differently in various situations. I suggested that the abuse he endured as a child might have led to the poor choices that brought us to this conversation. This tactic was successful in getting the individual to provide criminal admissions. It would not have been possible without a simple online search prior to the interaction.

OBSERVATIONS FROM SOMEONE'S PHYSICAL ENVIRONMENT

You can learn a great deal about a person by observing their physical surroundings. The space people create around themselves—what they display, collect, read, or even hide—offers valuable insight into who they are and what matters to them. This principle applies to homes, offices, locker rooms, and classrooms alike.

In my work in federal law enforcement, this concept came into play during the execution of search warrants. Observations made at the suspect's residence often provide invaluable clues. In these cases, being able to see another person's environment gives me a "CliffsNotes" version of what makes this person tick and key insights into their past behavior. Their books, video games, family photos, and team memorabilia all offer clues about their passions and worldview—clues that shape how I approach the conversation that will follow.

An example of this occurred while conducting a search warrant on a residence of an individual suspected of child exploitation. During the search, I noted the usual items: sports team memorabilia, hobby-related objects, and family photos. I briefly skimmed a few diary entries and drawings he had tucked under his bed. What caught my eye was a Bible on his bedside table, bookmarked to Matthew 14:22–33. This passage recounts Jesus's disciples crossing a lake in a boat, struggling against fierce winds and waves. Peter steps out of the boat to walk toward

Jesus, but upon feeling the strong gusts of wind, he becomes frightened and starts to sink. He cries out to Jesus, who immediately reaches out, catches him, and gently rebukes him for doubting. Some passages were highlighted, and words like "faith," "fear," and "trust" were scribbled in the margins. I wasn't sure how I would use this information, but it was clear he had been studying it recently.

The subject agreed to talk to me regarding allegations of child exploitation. I quickly established a rapport using information from his residence and social media accounts. About an hour into the conversation, he said, "I am a religious man; I would never hurt anyone." I avoid discussing religion and politics during all of my interactions. However, since he brought it up, I said, "Bob, you are a religious man, and we all fall short of the glory of God. This reminds me of a recent sermon about Peter in the book of Matthew. When Jesus called him out of the boat, he initially obeyed but then started to doubt as the wind and waves intensified. He began to sink, but Jesus reached out and saved him. I know you haven't been in this situation before and might be afraid. I want to offer you my hand to help navigate these waters."

This analogy led him to break down emotionally and confess to several instances of child exploitation. Although I caution against bringing up religion outside of church, in this case, it was the analogy he needed to hear.

Observing another person's environment can reveal what anchors them emotionally. Tactfully using that knowledge can accelerate trust and influence outcomes.

A CAUTIONARY TALE

Social media offers a powerful platform for connection and communication, but it also presents significant risks concerning your personal information. Scammers, identity thieves, or even potential romantic partners can easily exploit the details you share online.

Law enforcement has observed a sharp rise in identity theft cases linked to dating sites, where perpetrators pose as romantic interests. These scammers often target those who frequently share personal aspects of their lives on social media. What might seem to be harmless information provides these criminals with everything they need to craft a convincing fake persona.

Scammers typically approach their targets by pretending to share similar interests. With abundant information about the victim's preferences, dislikes, and hobbies, they can effortlessly mirror their interests. Like the Spotify effect discussed earlier, the scammer tunes in to the same "radio station" as the victim.

Over time, the scammer uses this false connection to extract even more personal information, eventually persuading the victim to send money, often under the guise of a "financial emergency." This is a real example of how the mirroring effect extends beyond body language into the digital realm. By imitating the victim's interests and lifestyle, the scammer creates a false sense of familiarity and trust, exploiting the connection. Even minor, innocent details can be pieced together by malicious individuals to build a profile that can be used against you. One of the ways to prevent this information from being used against you is to adjust the privacy settings to be more restrictive on your social media accounts. Many of the default settings are constructed in such a way that the company can monetize your private information.

Another concern arises when the person you're communicating with is aware of your online research. Be mindful that some websites, depending on your privacy settings, may notify users that you've viewed their activity. What starts as valuable information to help build rapport could quickly be perceived as intrusive or transactional, undermining your rapport-building efforts.

Now that we've examined how to gather and strategically use information before a conversation, let's take it a step further. In Part II, we'll uncover how to elevate first impressions and communication skills by tapping into the science behind our five senses and learning how to apply these insights in real-world interactions.

PART II

The Senses in Communication

Using All Your Senses to Build Trust and Influence

CHAPTER 4

Seeing Is Believing

"It's not what you look at that
matters, it's what you see."
—Henry David Thoreau

The first—and often most decisive—sense people use to assess you is vision. Before a word is spoken, your posture, expression, and attire send a signal: Are you competent? Are you trustworthy? Are you safe to open up to? From an evolutionary standpoint, sight was crucial for determining visual cues essential for survival. Today, although the context has shifted, visual assessment remains a fundamental part of human interaction. In this chapter, we will discuss the importance of your visual impact in establishing first impressions and enhancing communication.

As a Secret Service Agent, particularly during protective duties, one concept was consistently emphasized during our training: Always maintain an outward veneer of calm, especially during protective operations. No matter how stressful the situation is, the goal is to project a sense of calm and control. Frequently, during these operations, we are tasked with finalizing numerous details before the arrival of our protectee. It is incredibly stressful. However, I will never run or appear to be in distress. The old saying goes, "Never let them *see* you sweat." This will only keep you from making calm decisions, and this outward stress will become contagious. Imagine if the media saw a Secret Service Agent running toward the presidential limousine just before arrival. This would lead to the belief that something was not going according to plan and could lead to unease or panic among people in the area.

Similarly, flight attendants maintain steady composure during turbulence, thereby reassuring passengers through a calm demeanor. This intentional calmness is a well-rehearsed performance designed to inspire confidence and ease. Recently, I was traveling on a regional jet and sitting next to a college freshman who had never flown before. About halfway through the flight, we encountered significant turbulence. I noticed she was on the verge of a panic attack. I asked her if she was okay, and she responded, "Is the plane going to crash?"

I suggested that she quickly look down the aisle at the flight attendants and asked her to tell me what they were doing. She observed that they were sitting down, chatting, and laughing. I asked, "Do they *look* scared?" She said, "No." I replied, "If the experts who fly daily aren't scared, then we shouldn't be either." This calmed her instantly. Similar to how I was trained in the Secret Service, I realized that the flight attendants were also skilled at maintaining a calm exterior, which genuinely works.

Just as flight attendants maintain composure to reassure passengers, our outward presentation—including body language and attire—shapes how others perceive us. Confidence and competence are first communicated visually before a single word is spoken. Whether leading a conversation, negotiating a deal, or conducting an interview, our visual presence can instill confidence or create doubt. This presence is built on facial expressions, posture, and even the clothes we wear.

DRESSING FOR SUCCESS—THE POWER OF PROFESSIONAL ATTIRE

Dressing professionally has been scientifically proven to enhance a speaker's perceived credibility, competence, trustworthiness, authority, and self-confidence. Not only does professional attire impact how others perceive your credibility, but it also boosts your own confidence in that moment in time. As the famous quote by the football star Deion Sanders suggests, "If you look good, you feel good; if you feel good, you play good; if you play good, they pay good."

Studies have found that business attire significantly influences perceptions of a person's professionalism and capability. In most professional business settings, it is advisable to refrain from making bold fashion statements. Consider your audience and how your attire may impact the person you'll be speaking with. I always like to pose the following rhetorical question: If your spouse or children needed emergency lifesaving surgery, would you want the surgeon to wear unprofessional attire? What is the image you are putting out for others to view? If your position requires you to be perceived as competent, what you wear is extremely important.

I aim to dress slightly more formally than the person I am engaging with, striking a balance between professionalism and relatability. The goal is not to mirror their attire but to subtly project professionalism and competence. When I worked out of a field office with the Secret Service, I kept several outfits on hand to make quick adjustments. Agents learned early on that black or dark blue suits, paired with a white dress shirt, project authority and professionalism.

Color Choice in Attire

The color of our clothing during interactions can significantly impact how our message is perceived by others. Nature's bright colors provide some cautionary examples as we try to develop rapport and authentic connections with others. In the wild, vibrant hues primarily serve two crucial functions: warning others of potential danger and attracting mates for reproduction. For instance, the vivid colors of poison dart frogs signal toxicity to predators, while the flamboyant plumage of peacocks attracts potential mates.

Bright clothing, for instance, might inadvertently convey a sense of warning or attention-seeking, which can hinder open and comfortable dialogue. Overly vibrant attire may be perceived as aggressive or distracting, potentially making others feel uneasy or overshadowed. When I go without a suit jacket, I typically wear a soft blue dress shirt. Blue is widely recognized as a color that conveys trust, calm, and confidence.

The quality and fit of the clothing is also important. Too often, before a significant event requiring formal attire, individuals reach into their closet and select an outfit that worked well 20 pounds and 20 years ago. Unfortunately, it no longer fits properly, leading to an unprofessional and uncomfortable appearance. This discomfort often results in fidgeting, such as pulling at the neck of a tight shirt. This type of "venting" is a universal sign of anxiety. Ensuring your clothes fit well can help you avoid these distractions and project a more confident image.

One of my Secret Service colleagues became known for wearing a distinctive purple suit—ill-fitting and outdated. Despite his exceptional skills, the suit became a distraction, overshadowing his competence. When he finally invested in a well-tailored suit, the difference was striking—he immediately commanded more respect. This proved a hard truth: How you look sometimes matters just as much as your abilities.

Enclothed Cognition

Enclothed cognition is a term used to describe how what we wear can influence our thoughts and actions. This idea is essential in business, where factors like performance, decision-making, and professionalism are crucial. A study by Adam and Galinsky (2012) revealed that clothing is not just about appearances—it can impact how we think and work. For example, they discovered that people wearing lab coats, often associated with carefulness and precision, made fewer mistakes than those wearing painter's coats. This suggests that the meaning we attach to our clothing can affect our mental processes.[1]

A study published in the *Journal of Applied Psychology* explored how diverse types of clothing influenced workers' self-perception and productivity in a remote work environment. The research aimed to compare the effects of professional versus casual attire on factors such as focus, confidence, and overall productivity. Participants were divided into groups where one group wore professional attire, and the other wore casual clothing while performing work tasks remotely. Their productivity, self-perception (including confidence and professionalism), and even mood and engagement were assessed through self-reported surveys and performance tasks. The findings indicated that participants who wore professional attire reported higher focus, confidence, and perceived productivity than those in casual clothing. The study may have also highlighted that professional dress in a remote setting can reinforce a work-oriented mindset, leading to better task performance and engagement, thereby supporting the principle of enclothed cognition.[2]

When I have a video call requiring professional attire, I always steam my suit, press my shirt, shine my shoes, and even use a lint roller. These small details will not be noticeable on the other end of the call, but going through the process makes me feel more confident. It also helps me stick to my usual routine of getting ready, which reduces my anxiety and increases the likelihood that I'll perform well during the call.

Enclothed cognition also underscores the importance of routine and structure in business settings. Dressing for work, even when working from home, can act as a mental cue that it's time to start the day, helping to establish clear boundaries between work and personal time. As businesses adapt to remote or hybrid work models, understanding enclothed cognition can be crucial for keeping employees productive and professional. Encouraging employees to maintain some level of professional attire, even while working from home, could help them stay focused and maintain the same level of productivity they had in the office.[3]

This concept also plays a role in why US military drone pilots wear flight suits. Even though these pilots may be thousands of miles away from the drones they operate and are controlling them from secure buildings, the flight suit helps them mentally connect with the responsibilities and seriousness of their role, even though they are not physically in the cockpit. The flight suit enhances a pilot's sense of identity as part of the aviation community and reinforces the professionalism, discipline, and focus required for their duties. This psychological connection can improve their performance, decision-making, and attention to detail, critical when operating drones, especially in high-stakes or combat situations.

BODY LANGUAGE TECHNIQUES TO ENHANCE COMMUNICATION

Effective communication requires alignment between what we say, how we say it, and how we look while saying it. When these elements are out of sync, the disconnect is as jarring as a mismatched song and dance—something feels off, and our message loses its intended effect.

Research from experts like Joe Navarro underscores the power of nonverbal communication. Navarro, a former FBI agent specializing in body language, emphasizes that our gestures, facial expressions, and posture often reveal our true emotions, sometimes contradicting our chosen words. This incongruence can create confusion, skepticism, or distrust.[4]

Long before spoken language developed, early humans relied on body language—nonverbal communication—to communicate safety, intentions, and emotions. A relaxed posture, open hands, and friendly facial expression signaled nonthreatening intentions, while a rigid stance or narrowed eyes indicated potential danger. These instincts remain deeply embedded in our psychology today. We subconsciously assess whether someone's body language aligns with their words before deciding if we trust or believe them.

For instance, if a person says, "I'm happy to be here," but their arms are crossed, their shoulders are tense, and their facial expression is flat, the message feels insincere. Our brains prioritize visual and tonal cues over verbal ones—studies suggest that words alone make up only a small fraction of how meaning is conveyed. The majority of understanding comes from tone, pitch, facial expressions, and body positioning. Trying to understand how to read body language is a nuanced proposition. However, the following are specific tips and tactics you can use to make sure you project friendly signals and put yourself in the best position to communicate or influence effectively.

Eye Contact

Maintaining moderate eye contact is essential in establishing positive first impressions. Studies suggest maintaining eye contact for about 60–70% of the interaction time is optimal, striking a balance between engagement and comfort.[5]

A study found that direct gaze (eye contact) significantly increases feelings of connection and empathy between individuals. This research highlighted that eye contact helps to establish a deeper emotional bond and fosters trust and rapport.[6] This eye contact needs to stay out of that "creepy zone." Some younger individuals are not accustomed to elevated levels of eye contact. If they continue to look away, it doesn't necessarily mean they are being deceptive or disrespectful, but it is part of a generational shift regarding eye contact.

In professional interactions, I recommend that when you break eye contact, you look slightly upward or to the side rather than downward, especially in the early stages of a conversation. Looking down can project a lack of confidence, undermining your ability to establish authority and trust. However, there is one strategic moment when I intentionally break eye contact by looking downward—toward the end of a sensitive conversation, when I sense the individual is on the verge of making a disclosure. This subtle shift encourages them to mirror my behavior, which can help lower their resistance and create a less intimidating atmosphere, increasing the likelihood of them opening up.

With the surge in video calls following COVID, maintaining eye contact has become more critical than ever. However, a common issue arises during these calls: Most people look at their screens to view other participants while speaking. Since the camera is typically positioned at the top of the screen, this gives the impression that you're looking down, which can undermine the perception of confidence and strength.

On the other hand, if you try to look directly into the camera to simulate eye contact, you lose the ability to observe the facial expressions of the other participants in real time. This can be a significant disadvantage, as these expressions are vital to understanding whether your message is being received and agreed upon.

To address this, I use a product that lowers my video camera to the middle of the monitor. This setup allows me to maintain the appearance of direct eye contact with viewers while still being able to monitor their reactions in real time, striking the perfect balance between engaging with my audience and ensuring effective communication.

Another important aspect of eye contact is using "soft eyes." This refers to maintaining a relaxed and open expression when making eye contact. Think about your facial expression when you are straining to read the words on a page. Your expression might resemble contempt, which, as mentioned earlier, is a nonverbal conversation stopper. To avoid this, do the opposite—relax your eyes when making eye contact. This "soft" eye contact will make you appear more approachable, not creepy or contemptuous. When we struggle to hear or are intensely focused, we tend to furrow our brows and squint, unintentionally giving off signals of contempt or negativity. To prevent this, I ask people to imagine putting a piece of duct tape on their forehead—this mental image helps remind them to avoid displaying that negative expression.

The Eyebrow Flash

The timing of the eyebrow flash is critical, ideally occurring just before the initial handshake. This gesture signals genuine interest. Research shows that a quick eyebrow flash can enhance perceptions of warmth and approachability, often being interpreted as a friendly gesture that signals openness and receptivity. It also helps establish rapport and positive interactions by communicating a willingness to engage and connect, which is crucial for forming favorable first impressions.[7]

Understanding the concept of an eyebrow flash is crucial. An eyebrow flash is a quick, upward movement of the eyebrows, often accompanied by a brief widening of the eyes. It's important because it helps you avoid displaying contempt, which can quickly shut down a conversation. Showing facial expressions and body language associated with contempt is one of the fastest ways to cause a negative first impression and stifle dialogue. Even if we disagree with what the other person has done or is saying, we cannot outwardly express this if we want the conversation to continue. Your facial expressions should be like San Diego weather—80 degrees and sunny. Displaying even fleeting negative emotions can severely hinder communication.

The Importance of a Smile

A subtle smile is one of the most potent yet understated nonverbal cues that can significantly impact first impressions. This simple gesture conveys friendliness, and reassures the other party that you pose no threat. It transcends language barriers and is universally associated with positive emotions across cultures. It effectively conveys perceptions of warmth and approachability.[8]

Smiling offers a variety of psychological and social benefits. When we smile, our brains release endorphins and serotonin, neurotransmitters that foster feelings of happiness and reduce stress. This phenomenon was notably demonstrated during the 2024 Olympics when Kelsey Plum, a United States Women's Basketball Team player, was observed smiling before making crucial free throws in the game's final moments to secure the victory and the gold medal. Research supports the idea that smiling can significantly lower an individual's heart rate, contributing to physical and emotional well-being.[9] Not only does this help us feel better, but it also makes us appear more relaxed and approachable to others. Additionally, smiling is often contagious; when we smile at someone, they will likely smile back, which can initiate a cycle of positive interaction and mutual goodwill.

A smile combined with an eyebrow flash helps prevent us from curling our lips and narrowing our eyes, which are hallmarks of contempt. While contempt signals disdain and disapproval, a smile signals acceptance and approval.

In the instance of in-person customer service roles, smiling can improve customer satisfaction and create a positive experience. It can make customers feel valued and appreciated, leading to better outcomes and repeat business. However, smiling affects not just how people perceive us visually but also how they hear us. With telemarketing and customer service over the phone, it has long been known that smiling can increase sales and improve customer satisfaction surveys.

Head Nods

Nodding during a conversation is crucial as it shows you are listening and agreeing, which improves communication and builds rapport. Head nods are globally accepted as signs of attention and consent. By nodding, listeners show they are paying attention and agree with what is being said.

When listeners nod, speakers feel acknowledged. I can't tell you how important it is to observe head nods when teaching or providing a presentation. If I see audience members nodding, I get validation that I am providing valuable information and that it is being received. It is a nonverbal thumbs-up. When those nods stop or are nonexistent, the audience does not connect with the material.

Head nods have a marked influence on how much personal information people share. Nodding encourages people to talk by making the speaker feel at ease and validated. A study showed that therapists who engage in nodding and other forms of active listening tend to draw out more profound revelations from clients.[10] The nod must be slow and subdued to avoid looking like a bobblehead. It can't be nonstop nodding, or it loses its impact.

The Head Tilt

Another valuable nonverbal tool is a brief, subtle head tilt. Though seemingly minor, a subtle, well-timed head tilt can convey relaxation, attentiveness, and openness. Imagine during a conversation you are taking one of your ears and moving it two to three inches toward your shoulder for about one second. This is a gesture often associated with listening and engagement. When someone tilts their head during a conversation, it indicates that they are interested in and attentive to what the other person is saying. This slight movement can make the speaker feel heard and valued, encouraging them to open up and share more freely.[11]

One of the most compelling aspects of the head tilt is its implicit communication of trust and vulnerability. When we tilt our heads, we expose our carotid artery, a critical and vulnerable area of the body. This exposure is not just a physical action; it carries significant psychological implications. A study discussed how exposing the carotid artery subconsciously communicates trust and vulnerability. By tilting our heads, we signal to the other person that we feel safe and secure. Their research indicates that gestures like the head tilt can enhance perceptions of warmth and friendliness, making interactions more effective and enjoyable.[12]

As discussed with some of the other aspects of body language, head tilts need to be used randomly and briefly. Sometimes, my trainees utilize some of these practices, like head tilting, too frequently. It is as if they slept poorly and have a neck issue that needs to be addressed by the chiropractor. As in many things, use this tool as a spice, not a main dish.

Forward Lean

Maintaining an open posture with a slight forward lean can significantly enhance communication by conveying friendliness and genuine interest in the other person's message when transitioning to a seated setting. The forward lean is one of the most effective nonverbal cues for showing engagement and attentiveness in a conversation. A slight forward lean demonstrates attentiveness and interest in the conversation in which you are engaged. This subtle gesture signals to the speaker that you are fully present and engaged with what they are saying. When we lean forward, we communicate that we actively listen and value the other person's message.

Leaning forward during a conversation helps build rapport and trust, which are essential to effective communication. Studies show that forward-leaning posture is associated with increased perceptions of intimacy and rapport. When listeners lean forward, they create a sense of closeness and warmth, making speakers feel more comfortable and understood. Open and forward-leaning postures can lead to a greater willingness to share information. When an individual feels that their conversation partner is genuinely interested and empathetic, they are more likely to disclose personal thoughts and feelings.

We might think that leaning back and crossing our arms and legs shows a sense of coolness or relaxation. However, these postures are often viewed negatively as signs of disinterest, defensiveness, or arrogance. Leaning back can give the impression that you are disengaged or not taking the conversation seriously, which can hinder effective communication. On the other hand, a forward lean, combined with an open posture, projects warmth and approachability, making it easier for others to open up and share their thoughts and feelings.

Another benefit of a forward lean is that it facilitates conversation and is more closely aligned with a "confession posture." This posture closely aligns with a forward lean, where individuals subconsciously lean toward the person they confide in. This natural inclination to lean forward when sharing important or privileged information underscores the importance of this gesture in creating a safe and receptive communication environment. Adopting a similar posture can foster a sense of trust and openness, encouraging others to feel comfortable sharing sensitive information with you.

Open Posture

An open posture, characterized by uncrossed arms and legs, signals receptiveness and openness to dialogue. This posture is conducive to effective communication because it encourages the other party to perceive the speaker as approachable and engaged. It is a powerful tool for creating an inviting and supportive communication environment. When individuals adopt an open posture, they signal attentiveness, receptivity, and a willingness to engage. This nonverbal cue can have several positive effects on the interaction.

Open posture fosters a sense of trust and rapport between communicators. When people perceive openness in body language, they are more likely to feel safe and valued, encouraging them to share more personal and sensitive information. Nonverbal behaviors, such as maintaining an open posture, can significantly influence the degree of trust and rapport in an interaction. This is also closely aligned with research regarding ventral fronting. This involves facing another person directly with the torso and pelvis aligned toward them. This posture is interpreted as a signal of openness, interest, and engagement. When people engage in ventral fronting, it often indicates that they are comfortable and feel safe. When individuals face each other directly, they expose their vital organs (like the heart and abdomen), putting them in a vulnerable position.

Open posture can directly impact the likelihood of information disclosure. When people feel they are being listened to and understood, they are more inclined to reveal their thoughts, feelings, and experiences. This is particularly important in contexts such as counseling, therapy, and conflict resolution, where creating a safe and open environment is crucial for effective communication.

In contrast to open posture, closed posture can harm interpersonal communication. Closed posture is frequently interpreted as a sign of disinterest, hostility, or defensiveness. When individuals adopt a closed posture, they may unintentionally signal that they are not open to engaging in conversation or are emotionally distant. This can lead to misunderstandings and a communication breakdown.[13]

The defensive nature of a closed posture can create a psychological barrier to trust and openness. People are less likely to disclose personal or sensitive information if they perceive the listener as unapproachable or judgmental, which can hinder the development of a meaningful and productive dialogue.

Closed posture can also escalate tension and conflict in interpersonal interactions. When one party adopts a defensive stance, it can trigger similar responses in others, leading to a cycle of negative nonverbal cues exacerbating the conflict. This is extremely common during law enforcement interviews. Police officers are accustomed to having a defensive posture due to their training, which has them angle their bodies strategically to make themselves smaller targets. It often requires showing them a video of their defensive posture before the realization kicks in that their body language may be working against their de-escalation efforts in civilian encounters.

THE RIPPLE EFFECT OF EMOTIONS: EMOTIONAL CONTAGION AND MIRRORING

Emotions are contagious, and they can set the tone for any interaction. This ripple effect, known as **emotional contagion**, plays a crucial role in communication. For example, suppose you approach someone with crossed arms and a stern expression. In that case, they may unconsciously mirror this defensive posture—not because they are naturally defensive, but because they are reacting to your demeanor. Conversely, adopting a relaxed, open posture can invite the same in others, encouraging a more open and honest dialogue.

FACIAL EXPRESSIONS AND EMOTIONAL STATES

Facial expressions are potent ways we show our emotions. Psychologist Paul Ekman found that certain facial expressions are universal signs of happiness, sadness, anger, fear, surprise, and disgust.[14] These expressions give others a window into our current emotional state. However, they also can affect how we actually feel. When we make a facial expression, our brains get feedback from our facial muscles, which can strengthen the emotion we are expressing. This idea is called the facial feedback hypothesis. For example, you might feel happier if you force yourself to smile. Conversely, frowning can make you feel sad or angry.[15]

The combination of mirror neurons and facial expressions makes emotional contagion possible, where one person's mood can spread to others. Emotional contagion is significant in everyday conversations. When talking to someone, one person's mood can affect the whole conversation. A positive and enthusiastic person can make almost any conversation more enjoyable and productive. On the other hand, someone who is angry or frustrated can create tension and lead to misunderstandings and conflicts.

We can also benefit from having a slightly warm facial tone when conducting interviews. Negativity's contagion is highly counterproductive to establishing a good first impression and maintaining rapport. Emotional warmth attracts warmth from the person across from you and vice versa.

During sensitive communications, managing emotional contagion is crucial. When speaking with a person suspected of committing a crime, it is essential to focus on the issue at hand. If the interrogator shows negative facial expressions, it can cause the suspect to shift from short-term to long-term thinking. This shift can lead the suspect to think about the consequences of their actions, such as going to jail, which can hinder the disclosure process.

For example, when selling a car, dealerships often focus the buyer's attention on monthly payments instead of the total sticker price. This tactic promotes short-term thinking—making the purchase feel more affordable in the moment—while downplaying the larger long-term financial commitment. Early on in my career, I was involved in an investigation involving a suspect who was alleged to have committed a crime against one of the children in his care. The subject failed my polygraph examination, and I began to speak with him about his potential involvement. After about an hour of talking with the suspect, he confessed he had victimized the child in question. Immediately after the disclosure, a quick flash of contempt rushed across my face. All the acceptance and validation I had strategically used in the interaction was thrown out the window as he saw my disgust. This was a massive failure on my part. Despite obtaining the confession and being able to secure a conviction, I dropped my emotional mask, and the contempt I flashed caused the suspect to shut down. He had access to hundreds of children over the years. My inability to control my expressions from leaking out prevented me from being able to ask one of the most critical questions in these cases: "What else?"

Another example of failing to maintain emotional control occurred during a murder investigation in a Chicago suburb. My partner had been questioning the suspect for several hours, successfully building rapport and engaging in a productive conversation. However, when my partner casually remarked, "Hey, it's not like this kind of thing happened a whole bunch of times," the suspect's expression shifted from neutral to contempt, accompanied by an evident smirk, something famed psychologist Paul Ekman refers to as "duper's delight."[16] This unexpected reaction caused my partner to pause momentarily. The suspect's response implied something chilling: This was not his first murder. Although the suspect eventually confessed to the crime in question, providing graphic details, the chance to uncover additional victims or solve other murder cases was lost in those few seconds due to my partner's brief lapse in maintaining his poker face. To this day, my partner believes this individual, who is now serving a life sentence, is a serial killer.

In conclusion, while we often concentrate intensely on our word choice and articulation, we may need to consider how the other person receives our message. Although body language is not a definitive indicator of deception, it is a valuable tool for gauging the listener's response. Establishing a baseline understanding of someone's typical behavior can help us interpret their reactions during a conversation. In a job interview or negotiation, recognizing signs of disapproval—such as a frown, expressions of contempt, or pursed lips—enables us to assess the effectiveness of our communication in real time and adapt our approach as needed. Conversely, noticing positive cues, like someone lowering their head, leaning forward, or showing emotion, can indicate engagement. This awareness allows us to adjust our tone and volume, potentially steering the conversation toward a more favorable outcome, such as eliciting a critical admission or gaining agreement.

When asked which sense would be the most challenging to lose while still functioning in today's world, most people instinctively choose sight. However, hearing is just as vital. Now that we've explored the profound impact of vision on communication, let's examine the critical role of hearing and discover how to harness it as a powerful tool in our interactions.

CHAPTER 5

Hear Me Out

"We have two ears and one mouth so that we
can listen twice as much as we speak."
—Epictetus

What we say matters, but how we say it can determine whether our message is embraced or ignored. Think about the last time you heard a great speaker—their words alone are not what captivated you. Their vocal delivery—pitch, tone, volume, and pacing—made all the difference. From negotiations to interrogations, how we use our voice can establish authority, build rapport, or undermine credibility. In this chapter, we'll explore how vocal expression shapes perception, enhances influence, and strengthens communication.

THE IMPORTANCE OF SPEECH RATE, VOLUME, AND TONE IN EFFECTIVE COMMUNICATION

From an evolutionary perspective, long before formal language development, survival depended on our ability to interpret vocal cues. Before the advent of modern communication technologies like radios and telephones, early humans relied on these vocal signals to alert their groups—high-pitched sounds carried farther, cutting through open fields and dense forests to signal danger. This instinct persists today, as we subconsciously associate higher-pitched voices with fear, urgency, or uncertainty, while deeper voices project calmness, authority, and confidence.

Speakers with higher-pitched voices are often perceived as less confident and more anxious. Conversely, a lower-pitched voice signals confidence and authority, a phenomenon exploited in public speaking, broadcasting, and leadership.[1] One of my former partners, Lee, had a deep voice rivaling Morgan Freeman or James Earl Jones. In high-stakes situations, he didn't need to adjust his tone; his natural voice conveyed a sense of calm and conviction. However, I've found that slightly lowering my vocal pitch during intense moments—when anxiety is running high—helps me project confidence and authority to those I'm speaking with.

I vividly recall this from my first homicide case in 2003 during a polygraph examination. When the suspect failed the polygraph examination, and as I prepared to confront them about their involvement in the homicide, a surge of adrenaline caused my heart rate and breathing to spike. My voice pitch rose, and my speech rate exceeded 160 words per minute. The suspect quickly sensed the lack of confidence in my voice, leading to the abrupt end of the interview. Since then, I have researched vocal expression and utilized some of the following concepts significantly.

Speech Rate

Speaking too quickly can be perceived as a sign of stress or untrustworthiness. The optimal speaking rate of 120 to 130 words per minute enhances communication effectiveness by clearly expressing ideas and ensuring the message is understood. Speaking too fast can overwhelm listeners, leading to misunderstandings and decreased trust. On the other hand, speaking too slowly can cause listeners to lose interest. Thus, finding the right balance is crucial.[2]

Maintaining a moderate speech rate not only aids comprehension but also builds trust. Listeners are likelier to trust speakers who speak at a moderate pace, as it conveys confidence and calmness. This pace facilitates better comprehension, allowing listeners to engage more effectively with the content.[3]

However, stress often causes us to speak faster. When nervous, it is essential to consciously slow down. Frequently, when I am evaluating individuals during training sessions, they feel nervous conducting interviews while being evaluated. I emphasize the importance of consciously slowing their perceived speech rate, as adrenaline can accelerate their speech. When they later watched a video of the interaction, they often found that they spoke normally despite thinking they were slowing down.

In situations where someone speaks rapidly due to heightened energy, such as in discussions involving sensitive topics where the subject may be apprehensive of disclosing information, it is helpful to let them release that energy by talking. When it is your turn to speak, aim to maintain a slower rate and softer volume to ease the pressure in the conversation. You can always increase the intensity of your words later if needed, but starting too animated makes it challenging to tone down.

Volume Control

Adjusting your vocal volume is crucial for effective communication in various personal or professional contexts. We often encounter overly loud individuals, their voices echoing down hallways, which can be disruptive and off-putting in many situations. Conversely, speaking too softly risks being misunderstood and may convey a lack of confidence.

Lowering one's vocal volume, especially when discussing sensitive topics, can significantly impact communication dynamics by creating a sense of privacy and intimacy. This adjustment fosters trust and a feeling of safety, particularly during sensitive conversations. I have often had to utilize large rooms to conduct interviews in which we talked about extremely sensitive issues. Despite the size of a room, by lowering my volume, I can effectively shrink the size of the room and create perceived intimacy.

For example, if I'm speaking with an excitable individual who is talking loudly and rapidly, I intentionally slow my speech, lower my tone, and soften my volume. This deliberate adjustment will help de-escalate the situation and foster a calmer, more controlled conversation in many circumstances.

Lowering your vocal volume can dramatically enhance receptivity to your message and help build rapport. Moderating volume can also reduce listeners' defenses, making them more open to the speaker's message.[4] This technique, known as "vocal mirroring," involves matching the emotional tone and volume of communication to establish rapport and encourage openness.[5]

In my experience conducting thousands of interviews, I frequently use this technique when dealing with subjects who are under stress. Lowering my tone and speaking softly serves several purposes. It helps create a calming atmosphere, akin to the soothing voice that former FBI hostage negotiator Chris Voss describes as being used by late-night radio disc jockeys.[6] This approach conveys empathy and concern while reducing the perceived power imbalance between me and the subject.

I recall working alongside a detective on several criminal cases involving crimes against children. This detective had a recurring issue with volume control, something we've all encountered with a friend or colleague. His voice had a way of carrying down the hall, no matter where you were. Despite his deep expertise and interviewing prowess with both victims and suspects, his speaking volume was often too high, working against the environment of privacy we had tried to create.

The true impact of this became apparent during one particular case, which occurred the day after a World Series game where he had been cheering on his hometown St. Louis Cardinals. His voice was hoarse from all the shouting, and I remember handing him a cough drop before the interview. What followed was the best interview I had ever seen him conduct. With his voice softer and pacing slower, he projected a real sense of privacy and calm, creating a more conducive atmosphere. The result? A confession. His reduced volume made all the difference.

Furthermore, reducing vocal volume creates a perceived private space where individuals feel safe to disclose information. Adjusting volume creates an environment where the other party feels respected and heard, enhancing the quality of communication and mutual understanding.[7] Consider people commonly exchanging sensitive information: priests, therapists, and doctors. Can you remember any situation in which these individuals raised their voices in a professional setting? I dramatically lower my volume and deepen my tone when exchanging sensitive information and secrets. I may be in a public place, but I create an artificial sense of privacy.

Vocal Tone

Interpersonal communication is a complex mix of verbal and nonverbal signals, and vocal tone is a critical factor in how messages are received. Studies show that our brains pay more attention to how words are said than the actual words themselves. This finding highlights the importance of vocal tone in communication, especially in situations that involve high stakes, such as negotiations or interviews.

When I talk to a suspect in a case, I often use a positive tone instead of a flat or negative one. This strategy is based on research that shows that a cheerful voice can create favorable perceptions and increase the listener's responsiveness. The idea that you should talk to people over the phone with a smile reflects this principle; it communicates a noticeable positive mood even without visual signals. A positive tone and a slight smile generate a positive emotion and can leave a good impression on the other person. This is because vocal tone affects the listener's feelings and attitudes, often more strongly than the content of the message itself.[8]

A study published in the *Journal of the American Medical Association* (*JAMA*) showed that surgeons with better communication skills, including using a positive vocal tone, had significantly fewer malpractice claims.[9]

Margaret Thatcher, the former prime minister of the United Kingdom, underwent a notable transformation in her voice, adopting a deeper tone to project more authority and gravitas. Before this change, Thatcher faced widespread criticism, with media figures and comedy shows frequently caricaturing her voice. *The Guardian* described her voice as "a shrill, bossy woman," reflecting a common perception that her high-pitched tone undermined her leadership presence. A rival politician notoriously likened her voice to "fingernails scraping down a blackboard."[10]

To address these critiques, Thatcher sought the expertise of a professional vocal coach. She learned to control her voice consistently and maintain a lower pitch through various vocal exercises and breathing techniques. Additionally, she adopted a slower, more deliberate manner of speaking, which conveyed confidence and control.

This vocal transformation allowed Thatcher to project a more authoritative and commanding presence. Her deeper, steadier voice contributed to the perception of her as a strong and resolute leader, helping her gain respect and assert her position in a male-dominated political environment. Consequently, media portrayals of Thatcher became more favorable, emphasizing her strong leadership qualities rather than critiquing her for sounding shrill or overly emotional.[11]

In contrast, the story of Elizabeth Holmes, the former CEO of the now-bankrupt Theranos Corporation, serves as a cautionary tale. Holmes deliberately lowered her voice to project authority and credibility in the competitive, male-dominated Silicon Valley startup scene. However, like the manipulated results of Theranos's alleged successes, her altered voice was not sustainable. In personal settings or when intoxicated, Holmes's vocal tone would change dramatically.[12] We have also all seen videos where politicians, consciously or unconsciously, attempt to match the speaking mannerisms of another group to which they do not belong. Regardless of intent, this is universally despised. This underscores that alterations in vocal tone, pacing, and body language should be subtle to be compelling and authentic.

The lesson here is that Margaret Thatcher strategically lowered her voice to project authority, using professional coaching to develop a deeper, more controlled tone. Her shift was gradual and sustainable. In contrast, Elizabeth Holmes artificially lowered her voice to cultivate an image of credibility. However, when she let her guard down, her natural tone resurfaced, exposing the inauthenticity of her persona. This highlights a crucial lesson: Adjusting one's voice for authority must take place over a period of time and be natural or it risks backfiring.

I am from the Midwest and have a very neutral speaking tone and rate. This is one reason many news and radio personalities are from the Midwest. This lack of an accent and standard speaking rate appeals to a broad audience. It also allows me to adjust slightly to the person I am talking to. I would slightly increase my speaking rate when interviewing people in the Northeast. In the South, I would typically slow it down. However, these adjustments must be subtle.

Varying Pitch and Tone for Interest and Calm

Varying vocal pitch and tone is another crucial aspect of effective communication. A monotone voice can cause listeners to lose interest, similar to the trademark nondescript "wah-wah" sound of Charlie Brown's teacher. Studies have shown that people perceive those who vary their pitch and tone as more engaging and charismatic.[13] During challenging conversations, it is essential to recognize that the other person may be experiencing stress, triggering a fight-or-flight response. To soothe them, use body language and modulate your voice's pitch, pace, and tone. Lowering your vocal tone can help shift the nervous system from a fight-or-flight response to a more relaxed state, reducing heart rate and cortisol levels. This physiological calming can lead to better cooperation and recall.

IMPORTANCE OF VOCAL WARM-UPS

Vocal warm-ups are crucial for enhancing the flexibility of the vocal folds. They allow speakers to achieve a broader range of pitch and vocal tone, resulting in a warmer, clearer voice that effectively captures listeners' interest. Scientific research supports that warming up the voice reduces strain on the vocal cords, enabling prolonged periods of speaking without discomfort or damage.[14]

Just as athletes warm up their muscles, professional speakers warm up their voices. Humming, deep breathing, and tongue twisters improve vocal clarity. Personally, before a big presentation or lengthy interview,

I drink honey-infused tea and use a menthol throat lozenge. The menthol clears nasal passages, giving me more vocal range, while the honey soothes my throat—small adjustments that can make a big impact. If world-class singers warm up before performing, why wouldn't we do the same for high-stakes conversations?[15]

Our voice is a tool of influence that can create trust, establish authority, or even uncover deception. From pitch to pacing, every element of vocal delivery shapes how we are perceived. But communication doesn't end with what we say or how we say it—it extends to every sense we use.

VOICE IMPROVEMENT APPLICATIONS

One of the most effective tools I've used to enhance my vocal tone, pacing, pitch, and inflection has been dedicated voice training applications. These programs, which are on my smartphone, are specifically designed to strengthen vocal range, control, and clarity, all of which are essential for persuasive and confident communication. I've personally incorporated this into my daily routine, and the results have been both noticeable and lasting—not just to me, but to those receiving my message. With just 5 to 10 minutes of consistent practice each day, you can significantly elevate the quality and impact of your voice.

SILENCE AS A WEAPON IN COMMUNICATION

Mark Twain once said, "The right word may be effective, but no word was ever as effective as a rightly timed pause." Pauses are more than just breaks in speech—they create anticipation, allow key points to land, and reduce the need for filler words like "um" and "ah."[16] In negotiations, pauses can shift pressure onto the other person, prompting them to speak first. In interviews, silence encourages disclosure as people rush to fill the void. The power of silence lies not in what is said, but in what is left unsaid.

When discussing the effectiveness of communication, we often overlook the profound impact of silence. Silence is a powerful tool, particularly in contexts where the goal is to elicit information. Research and practical experience in psychology, negotiation, and interviewing has demonstrated that the strategic use of silence can encourage people to disclose more information than they might otherwise.

People find silence uncomfortable in social interactions. This discomfort can create pressure to fill the gap, leading individuals to continue speaking to break the silence. This phenomenon, known as the "awkward silence" effect, often prompts people to divulge more than they initially intended. Studies have found that conversational gaps frequently lead to increased self-disclosure as individuals seek to alleviate the discomfort of silence.[17]

Silence can be a powerful indicator of active listening and patience. When an interviewer or conversational partner does not immediately respond, it signals that they are genuinely interested in what the speaker has to say. This can create a safe environment where the speaker feels valued and understood, encouraging them to share more openly.

Therapists also use silence to give clients space to think and reflect, often leading to more profound self-disclosures and therapeutic breakthroughs. Studies have shown that patients provided more detailed information when physicians allowed for pauses and did not rush to fill the silence, promoting a sense of introspection and thoughtfulness.[18]

In my experience with thousands of interviews, I have seen the power of silence firsthand. I often use silence to make suspects uncomfortable, prompting them to fill the communication void with additional information. Trainers who focus on negotiations commonly emphasize this tactic, where silence pressures the other party into speaking more, revealing their true intentions or additional helpful information.

Having explored the power of sound, it's time to examine another underappreciated sense in communication: touch. Let's uncover how physical interaction, from handshakes to spatial awareness, impacts how we connect and persuade.

CHAPTER 6

The Midas Touch

"The handshake of the host affects
the taste of the roast."
—Benjamin Franklin

The power of touch is undeniable when it comes to influencing people. Haptics, the science of touch, has been used for centuries to create positive effects on individuals. In this chapter, we will examine recent research regarding the importance of touch and illustrate how to apply it to improve communication, relationships, and overall well-being.

Touch is one of the most powerful yet delicate tools for communication. When used with intention and care, it can break barriers and ease tension. In my professional interactions, I've employed touch strategically—through confident handshakes during introductions and departures and a strategic touch on someone's shoulder when they are in emotional distress.

I'll never forget one instance during a homicide investigation in the Chicago area where my partner and I were assisting the local police. The suspect was accused of the heinous crime of strangling a young woman. In the interrogation room, he teetered on the edge of confession, caught in a mental tug-of-war between his conscience and the crushing reality of life in prison. At this pivotal moment—what I call the "moment of truth"—he was metaphorically shifting between short-term and long-term thinking, knowing what he *should* do but hesitating to pay the steep price.

Sensing the tension, I moved closer and gently placed my hand on his shoulder. For a few seconds, I left it there. I could almost feel the weight of the situation pressing down on him, his resolve beginning to crumble. That touch was like a hot liquid meeting a sugar cube—softening, melting away the last of his defenses. It was the connection he needed to take the final step and confess to his crime.

When wielded with precision and empathy, touch can be transformative. It bridges gaps that words cannot, offering support, presence, and understanding in the moments that matter most. When used correctly, touch becomes an invaluable tool for connecting on a profoundly primal level.

However, why does touch have such a powerful impact on us? We must look back to our evolutionary ancestors—chimpanzees—to understand its importance. In chimp communities, grooming serves a critical role beyond just hygiene. Grooming is an act of bonding, reassurance, and social connection. It solidifies relationships within the group and fosters trust. For chimps, the physical act of touch through grooming is essential to their tribal cohesion, helping maintain peace and harmony within their community.

Humans, like our primate relatives, have an instinctual connection to touch. The tactile connection we feel during a handshake or a reassuring pat on the back taps into something deeply tribal. Just as chimps groom one another to build trust, humans use touch to break down social barriers, establish rapport, and create a sense of belonging.

In today's digital age, where so much of our communication happens through screens and devices, the importance of touch is often overlooked. However, in person-to-person interactions, it remains one of our most powerful tools. Touch can communicate empathy, sincerity, and warmth—all essential elements in building relationships, whether in a business setting, during an interview, or in everyday life.

Incorporating touch into your communication repertoire must be done with care and cultural sensitivity, but when used appropriately, it can deepen trust and improve the overall quality of your interactions. Just as the chimps' grooming ritual is crucial to their social fabric, our modern understanding of touch offers a pathway to connection that transcends words.

The power of touch in communication is deeply embedded in human physiology. It directly influences our emotions and social bonds by releasing specific neurochemicals. Understanding these hormones helps explain why touch can build trust, reduce stress, and foster meaningful connections.

Often called the "connection chemical," oxytocin is released during physical touch and is vital in promoting trust, empathy, and bonding. Enhancing oxytocin levels can create a sense of closeness and security, making interactions feel more genuine and impactful. Boosting oxytocin in ourselves and those we engage with improves communication by fostering contentment, reducing anxiety, and enhancing emotional stability. You can think of this process as making deposits in a "trust bank account"—just as you save money for financial stability, you "deposit" oxytocin to nurture trust-based relationships.

Touch also triggers the release of endorphins and dopamine, neurotransmitters associated with feelings of pleasure and reward. These chemicals boost mood and well-being, making touch a powerful tool for positive reinforcement and stress relief.

Physical touch has been shown to lower cortisol levels, the hormone associated with stress. Lower cortisol levels contribute to reduced anxiety and a calmer state of mind, essential for effective communication. By helping to reduce cortisol, touch can help foster a more relaxed, open, and engaging interaction, providing a calming effect in communication.

Interestingly, oxytocin metabolizes much more quickly than cortisol. This poses a challenge: Once stress is introduced into a conversation and cortisol is released, it takes a significantly higher amount of oxytocin to return to a baseline of calm and trust. This imbalance means restoring a positive dynamic requires extra effort once stress enters the equation. For this reason, focusing on practices that promote oxytocin release and minimize cortisol production is essential for maintaining a productive and positive communicative environment.

GUIDELINES FOR USING TOUCH IN CONVERSATIONS

When engaged in sensitive conversations, it is essential to use touch strategically:

Handshake at Greeting: A great handshake can set a positive tone for the interaction.

Light Touch to Gain Attention: A slight touch on the hand or shoulder can help direct attention and shift the person into listening mode.

Comforting Touch: A light touch on the shoulder can provide comfort when the person is emotional.

Handshake at Conclusion: Ending with a handshake can reinforce the connection and signify the conclusion of the interaction.

INDIVIDUAL PREFERENCES

In addition to cultural considerations, individual preferences play a significant role in how touch is perceived. Some people are more comfortable with physical touch than others, and it is essential to be sensitive to these preferences. Observing nonverbal cues and seeking verbal consent, when necessary, can help ensure that touch is welcomed and appreciated. Early in my career, my partner Brian and I conducted a homicide polygraph on a suspect serving a life sentence. The environment was challenging, a high-security prison, and the suspect was highly antisocial. He was very withdrawn when I shook his hand, indicating his discomfort. During the initial portion of the interview, I lightly touched his arm to emphasize a point subtly. He immediately flashed a facial expression of contempt and made a fist with his other hand. Recognizing his discomfort, I refrained from further touch. This incident highlights the importance of being attentive to nonverbal cues and respecting personal boundaries.

THE WORLD'S GREATEST HANDSHAKE

An effective handshake is crucial to making a positive first impression and conveying charisma. Conversely, a poor handshake can leave a negative impression. A cold, clammy, and weak handshake is universally viewed unfavorably. To prepare for an important or high-profile interview, I take several steps to ensure my handshake is positive.

Managing Sweaty Palms: Anxiety can cause sweaty palms, so I carry antiperspirant in my briefcase and spray my hands before the interaction begins. This keeps them dry and free from embarrassing moisture.

Warming Cold Hands: To avoid chilly hands, I aggressively rub my hands together for 10–15 seconds before entering the room. When conducting a polygraph, I use a portable hand warmer. If seated, you could also briefly place your palm under your leg if you anticipate an upcoming handshake, which will warm your hands slightly. It is crucial not to let the other person see you drying or warming your hands, as this can reveal your nervousness.[1]

Handshake Technique: Aim to connect at the navel level, equidistant from the other person, to create a sense of balance and equality. Keep the handshake concise with one shake, a short hold, and prompt disengagement. A good technique is less of a handshake and more of a brief "handhold." Briefly break eye contact to ensure a good connection with the other person's hand, then quickly reestablish eye contact to show attentiveness and establish a sense of connection.

Grip Firmness: Aim for a firm, confident handshake without applying excessive pressure. Many people understand the problem with a very limp handshake but overcompensate and utilize a death grip that is also perceived poorly.[2]

Grip Alignment: One often overlooked aspect of a good handshake is the slight clockwise tilt of the hand toward the one or two o'clock position.

A bit more on grip alignment: This has two key benefits, one primal and the other related to modern habits. Understanding the significance of the palm's lighter color is crucial in a handshake. Due to a thicker skin layer, lower melanin levels, and less sun exposure, this natural trait can subtly signal to the other person that you are unarmed, fostering a sense of openness and trust.

Secondly, modern office work and driving often keep our hands in a pronated position. This is our natural and preferred alignment, as you can observe by standing straight with your hands naturally resting at your sides, palms facing your thighs. Positioning your hand slightly clockwise during a handshake allows the other person to connect in a comfortable, familiar, pronated position.

This subtle adjustment with your grip alignment makes a handshake feel more natural and allows the other person to feel a sense of control—an often-unspoken factor in forming a first impression.

As a result of the primacy and recency effect, people place more weight on an interaction's initial and final impressions. A handshake will very often occur at both these points of time and, as a result, play a crucial role in the overall impact of the interaction. A great handshake is a skill that carries immense value in various professional settings. By following these tips—preventing wetness and coldness and mastering grip firmness and alignment—you can ensure your handshake makes a lasting impression.[3]

A handshake may be an interaction's first and final act, but its impact lingers. Touch builds trust and strengthens relationships, making it invaluable in personal and professional settings. Just as touch influences how we perceive and connect with others, our senses of smell and taste shape our emotions in ways we rarely notice. In the next chapter, we'll uncover how these often-overlooked senses silently guide our interactions—and how you can use them to your advantage.

CHAPTER 7

Aromas and Appetites

"Taste and smell are our oldest senses, and they connect us in an intimate, primal way to the world around us."
—Diane Ackerman

Imagine walking into a bakery on the way into work—the rich aroma of fresh bread and cookies instantly makes you feel at home. However, you arrive at work and are greeted with the smell of your musty, stale office—suddenly, your mood shifts. Smell and taste operate in the background of our interactions, quietly influencing our emotions, decisions, and even trust levels. Smell and taste, though often overlooked, can be critical for influencing perception and making people comfortable during an interaction.

Subtle scents are so powerful that they can alter our spending habits without us realizing it. In a 2006 German study, gamblers spent over 40% more when a pleasant aroma filled the casino. The scent worked below conscious awareness, proving that smell is an invisible influencer.[1]

Taste has a powerful yet often unnoticed influence on our emotions and decisions. Have you ever taken a sip of bitter, lukewarm coffee and felt an unexpected wave of irritation? Or indulged in a piece of chocolate and suddenly felt more at ease? It's not just in your head—taste has a direct line to our emotions and even our decision-making.

Researchers at the University of Chicago found that drinking something bitter before evaluating ethical dilemmas made participants significantly harsher in their judgments. Imagine how this unconscious bias plays out in negotiations, interviews, or even first dates—the taste in your mouth may shape the judgments you don't even realize you're making.[2] These findings highlight a crucial truth: While sight and sound take center stage in communication, smell and taste function like background processes in a computer. Just as hidden algorithms influence your device's speed and overall performance without you noticing, these senses quietly shape your emotions and decisions—often before you're even aware of their impact.

Unlike other senses, smell is directly linked to memory and emotion. A familiar perfume can evoke nostalgia, and the scent of home-cooked food can transport us to childhood. Smell bypasses rational thought and taps directly into instinct, making it a key player in trust-building and influence. Businesses and salespeople leverage these effects—whether it's the aroma of coffee in a bookstore aimed at increasing sales or a real estate agent's strategic use of freshly baked cookies at an open house to make it feel like a home.

In this chapter, we explore how smell influences first impressions and information disclosure.

THE SIGNIFICANCE OF SMELL

In the animal kingdom, scent serves as a crucial alert to prey about the presence of predators. Similarly, smell can be pivotal in shaping first impressions in human interactions. Applying a touch of fragrance or perfume can help start interactions on a positive note, ensuring no distracting or unpleasant odors. Neglecting aspects like body odor or foul breath can shift the focus from the conversation and project an unprofessional image.

Personal Hygiene and Smell

Personal hygiene is crucial for creating positive first impressions. For instance, body odor or bad breath can be significant distractions during interactions, leading to negative perceptions. I once had to talk with my high school-aged son about his generous use of body spray and cologne, emphasizing that "less is more." What you may think is a pleasant smell can be highly distracting to someone else. Staying neutral regarding your scent profile is more important than expressing yourself with a signature scent. Neutral scents help maintain focus on the interaction itself rather than on potentially overpowering fragrances, ensuring that communication remains clear and effective.

Being mindful of the scent of one's breath is crucial but often overlooked. Encounters with individuals who have bad breath can make it challenging to focus on their words. Keeping track of breath freshness is advisable to avoid being on the receiving end of such an experience. Since chewing gum might seem unprofessional, I opt for portable, disposable toothbrushes in my briefcase for a quick and discreet refresh before interactions. This simple practice not only ensures fresh breath but also boosts my self-confidence.

The Psychological Impact of Smell

Smell is closely tied to emotions and memory. Specific scents can elicit powerful emotional responses, triggering memories that influence how we feel about a person. Pleasant or familiar odors can create positive associations, enhancing our overall impression of someone, while unpleasant smells may evoke discomfort or aversion. The connection between smell and memory is evident in how our brains can vividly recall the aroma of a favorite meal, highlighting the strong emotional ties associated with smell.[3]

Research has shown that the olfactory system is directly connected to the brain's limbic system, which is responsible for emotions and memory.[4] This connection explains why certain smells can trigger vivid memories and emotional responses. For instance, the smell of freshly baked cookies might remind someone of their grandmother's kitchen, evoking feelings of comfort and warmth.

The Role of Environmental Smells

Smell's influence extends beyond personal hygiene to the environment in which interactions occur. Pleasant scents in a room can enhance the mood and improve the quality of communication. Research demonstrates that environments with pleasant odors lead to more positive judgments and perceptions. This underscores the importance of ensuring that the spaces where interactions occur are free from unpleasant odors and infused with subtle, pleasing scents.[5]

Consideration of the environment is equally important. In my experience, many police interview rooms are far from optimal environments for information exchange. Simply removing odor from the environment is a significant enhancement in these settings. In a past case, I was assisting a local police department with a polygraph examination as a part of a homicide investigation. The interview room I utilized was the only one available, and suspects and detectives almost always occupied it. As a result, the room had become a buffet of unique scents. The lingering odor of stale beer, urine, and body odor permeated the space.

During my interview, my partner and I were on the verge of a breakthrough—possibly a confession. Then I saw the suspect look around, wrinkle his nose, and mutter, "This room smells like prison." In that instant, his mind shifted from short-term thinking (*Should I confess?*) to long-term consequences (*This is where I'll end up if I confess*). His body language changed, and his willingness to talk evaporated. The interrogation was effectively over—not because of my approach, but because of an unconscious trigger embedded in the room itself.

Many hotels, spas, high-end retailers, and coffee shops have recognized the profound impact of subtle aromas on enhancing the customer experience. Research has consistently shown that specific scents can significantly influence mood, cognition, and physical responses, making them valuable tools for creating welcoming and enjoyable atmospheres.

A study found that lavender aromatherapy significantly reduced anxiety in patients awaiting dental treatment. Patients exposed to lavender reported lower anxiety levels compared to those not exposed to the scent, highlighting lavender's calming properties.[6] Lavender is not the only scent with powerful properties.

> **Sandalwood, Vanilla:** Studies have demonstrated that these scents significantly reduce stress and anxiety levels. Test subjects exposed to these aromas reported feeling more relaxed and at ease, making these scents ideal for creating soothing environments.[7, 8]
>
> **Citrus (Lemon, Orange, Grapefruit):** Citrus scents, particularly lemon, have been found to enhance mood and increase alertness. Research indicates that exposure to citrus aromas can improve cognitive performance and uplift mood, providing a fresh and invigorating feeling.[9]
>
> **Peppermint, Eucalyptus, Cinnamon:** These scents have been shown to energize and focus individuals. Studies suggest that spaces infused with peppermint and eucalyptus are perceived as more welcoming and stimulating, enhancing mental alertness and the overall atmosphere.[10]

These findings underscore the power of scent in shaping human experiences. By carefully selecting and incorporating specific aromas, businesses can create environments that appeal to the senses and promote relaxation, alertness, and positive emotions. The strategic use of scents is a subtle yet effective way to enhance interactions.

Now, let us examine the impact that taste has on communications.

THE SIGNIFICANCE OF TASTE

Taste might seem like one of the least significant senses during initial interactions or difficult conversations. However, if we reflect on our own lives, many vital conversations occur during meals. Family dinners have been a staple for communication since childhood, and significant life events—proms, weddings, anniversaries—are often marked with shared meals. Research supports the notion that shared food experiences can enhance cooperation and collaboration. Sharing food promotes a sense of unity and mutual trust, facilitating smoother interactions.[11]

The Evolutionary Basis of Eating Together

Sharing meals is an ancient practice that has become fundamental to human social interaction. In prehistoric times, communal eating was essential for survival, fostering group cohesion and cooperation.[12] This tradition continues today, where meals are opportunities for social bonding and communication. Eating together triggers the release of endorphins and oxytocin, enhancing trust and empathy.[13]

Eating together can significantly impact the psychological dynamics of communication. Research indicates that sharing meals fosters a sense of camaraderie and reduces perceived power imbalances.[14] For example, sharing a meal with colleagues in professional environments can break down hierarchical barriers, promoting more open and honest communication.

Case Study: Using Food to Facilitate Difficult Conversations

During a significant child exploitation investigation, I interviewed both primary suspects after examining their social media activity. Notably, each had a favorite fast-food restaurant—one preferred Wendy's, the other McDonald's. I saw an opportunity to use this information strategically, leveraging it to build rapport and ease their anxiety.

Before heading to the police department, I made some regrettable dietary choices. Starving, I stopped at a gas station where my options were far from ideal. With little else available, I reluctantly grabbed two buffalo chicken mini burritos that had been endlessly rotating on the infamous roller grill, washing them down with a strong energy drink. I had anticipated having more time to prepare, but upon arrival, I was told the interviews needed to begin immediately.

In my professional experience, difficult conversations often unfold more smoothly over food or drinks. Eating naturally fosters a more relaxed atmosphere, making individuals less defensive and more open to dialogue. This principle is rooted in biology—mammals in a heightened state of stress generally won't eat. I've found that offering food serves as both a rapport-building tool and a barometer of anxiety. If a suspect refuses, it often indicates they're still in fight-or-flight mode, signaling that I need to work further to put them at ease before proceeding.

In the first interview, I casually mentioned my hunger and suggested grabbing something from Wendy's, offering to bring back food for the suspect. He requested a cheeseburger, large fries, and diet soda. Mirroring his order, I deliberately pulled cash from my wallet in front of him before asking the lead detective to pick up the food. This subtle act established a dynamic of reciprocity—he saw me spending my own money on his meal. As we ate, his anxiety visibly diminished, and soon after, he began making admissions. He ultimately confessed to several acts of predatory child abuse.

I tailored my approach similarly for the second interview. Knowing this suspect favored McDonald's, I repeated the process. Again, I casually mentioned my hunger and offered to pick up food. She eagerly requested a Big Mac, large fries, and soda. As before, sharing a meal created a sense of familiarity and comfort, helping her anxiety melt away. Within a short time, she provided a full confession detailing horrific acts of child abuse.

While my stomach—and waistline—weren't exactly grateful for the gas station burritos and fast-food meals, the results were undeniable. A simple meal had been enough to break down psychological barriers, disarming these individuals just enough for them to open up.

Research suggests that the multisensory experience of sharing a meal can create a more profound connection between individuals, enhancing empathy and trust. This principle was evident as both suspects became more open and cooperative during our shared meals.[15] Interestingly, during a recorded jail call, the second suspect admitted to their mother that the only reason they confessed was because they got McDonald's during our interaction. This anecdote underscores the effectiveness of using shared meals as a rapport-building strategy. However, this is a universal concept, as anyone in corporate America knows that million-dollar deals are routinely negotiated during business lunches or at the county club dining room after 18 holes of golf.

The physiological effects of eating can also reduce anxiety. When a person eats, their parasympathetic nervous system is activated, which counteracts the body's stress responses.[16] This shift can make individuals feel safer and more willing to open up. Offering food to someone during a stressful situation can thus help calm them down and make them more receptive to communication.

So, what are the tangible benefits of using food and refreshments to help facilitate communication? Here are a few scientifically backed strategies.

Facilitating Difficult Conversations: Next time you need to have a tough conversation, don't just sit across from someone—sit *with* them over a meal. The act of eating together shifts the dynamic from confrontation to collaboration.

Creating a Sense of Reciprocity: Offering someone a drink or snack may seem like a small gesture, but it taps into a fundamental human instinct—reciprocity. If I buy you a coffee, you're more likely to be receptive to what I have to say. This act can make the other person feel valued and respected, fostering more honest and open communication.

Using Food as an Icebreaker: Starting conversations about food preferences or recent dining experiences can be an effective icebreaker.

This can help establish common ground and make the conversation more personal and engaging.

Incorporating pleasant food experiences into conversations can create positive associations that enhance the overall interaction. This can be particularly useful in building long-term relationships and fostering loyalty. Eating together can improve empathy and understanding between individuals. Research suggests that shared experiences, including meals, can lead to greater empathy and a deeper understanding of each other's perspectives. This can be particularly valuable in settings where cooperation and collaboration are essential.[17]

Whether it's the subtle scent of a room or the taste of a meal shared during an interaction, these often-overlooked senses play a crucial role in human connection. Strategically incorporating scent and taste can subtly shape emotions, build trust, and enhance communication. But while our senses influence perception, they are only one piece of the puzzle.

The timing and environment of an interaction are just as critical—the same words can have drastically different effects depending on *when* and *where* they are spoken. With a deeper understanding of how all our senses impact interpersonal communication, learning to choose the right moment and setting can significantly enhance the effectiveness of any interaction.

PART III

Strategic Communication & Influence

Timing, Mindset, Influence, and Listening

CHAPTER 8

The Right Place at the Right Time

"It's not enough to be in the right place at the right time. You have to be the right person in the right place at the right time."
—T. Harv Eker

Crafting an environment conducive to positive interactions and picking the right time to engage in a conversation is pivotal, especially in settings where anxiety and stress levels are typically high. This chapter will examine ways in which we can alter the environment and timing to put ourselves in a position to have a higher likelihood of a positive outcome, whether during a business lunch, job interview, or even a date.

DESIGNING A CALMING ENVIRONMENT

Few places create more anxiety than a dentist's office. The sound of drills, the smell of antiseptic, and the sight of sharp instruments are enough to make anyone uneasy. Dentists, aware of this, strategically design their offices to minimize stress. They play soothing music, offer distractions like TV screens, and sometimes even use aromatherapy to create a calming atmosphere.

Why? Because comfort leads to cooperation. Relaxed patients are likelier to trust their dentist and endure necessary procedures without resistance. The same principle applies to communication—if people feel at ease, they're more likely to engage openly and honestly. Whether it's a sales pitch, an interrogation, or a difficult conversation, setting up the right environment is just as important as what you say.

A thoughtfully designed dentist's office goes beyond mere aesthetics; it incorporates strategic elements to create an atmosphere that minimizes stress and maximizes comfort. A private lobby serves as a physical buffer, shielding patients from the audible sound of dental instruments, and as a psychological sanctuary, fostering a sense of tranquility. For those undergoing more extensive procedures, providing a discreet exit is a nod to the importance of privacy, underscoring a commitment to personalized and considerate care.

The waiting area emerges as a pivotal space where patients are afforded choices to exert control over their surroundings, thereby alleviating anxiety. From a curated selection of magazines to open Wi-Fi and the therapeutic presence of a serene aquarium, the array of distractions is designed to cater to diverse preferences. Even the youngest patients find solace in designated gaming consoles, offering a tailored and comforting escape. Additionally, the availability of an array of coffees and teas injects a touch of warmth and personalization into the waiting experience.

Transitioning into the examination room, the focus on patient comfort persists. The examination space's color palette and ergonomic design create a private and calming sanctuary. Patients are empowered with choices, be it the option to watch television or select from a range of radio stations, reinforcing a sense of agency. Even routine aspects, such as the fluoride flavor or the toothbrush's color, are transformed into opportunities for personalization and empowerment.[1]

CONTROL THE ENVIRONMENT

Creating an environment conducive to communication involves several key elements, including room location, size, temperature, and lighting. Each of these factors can significantly impact participants' comfort levels and the quality of the interaction.

Room Location

The location of the room where you are about to engage in sensitive communications should be convenient and easily accessible yet discreet enough to ensure privacy. A room away from high-traffic areas can minimize noise and interruptions, creating a more controlled environment for conversation. In the interview rooms we design for law enforcement, we try to use soundproofing material in the room design. This creates a sense of privacy in cases involving both victims and witnesses.

Room Size

A space that's too small can create a sense of confinement, making participants feel trapped or uneasy. In a cramped room, people may unconsciously adopt defensive body language—crossed arms, leaning back, or angling their bodies away from others—which can impede trust and rapport building. The lack of personal space can create physical and psychological discomfort, leading to heightened tension and even the potential for anxiety or a fight-or-flight response, which works against productive dialogue.

Conversely, a room that is too large can feel impersonal, amplifying the distance between participants. When a conversation occurs in a vast or sparsely furnished room, the physical gap can contribute to a psychological gap, making people feel isolated and less connected. This room size can create an environment where people must project their voices just to be heard. This can cause people to step outside their normal vocal range and cause privacy to suffer due to the increased volume. We need to be aware that people don't yell their secrets; they whisper them. Sometimes, I am forced to interview a subject in a large conference room. When this happens, I will position the desk and chairs to create a separate, smaller space within the room to make the subject more comfortable.

Ideally, a medium-sized room creates a balanced environment that promotes comfort and focus. The seating should be arranged thoughtfully, preferably in an inviting but not overly close way, allowing people to maintain their personal space while still engaging fully. Comfortable chairs positioned at an appropriate distance foster an atmosphere where individuals feel secure yet connected, encouraging them to open up without feeling crowded or exposed.

Room Temperature

Maintaining a comfortable room temperature is essential for helping participants feel at ease. Rooms that are too hot or cold can be distracting and uncomfortable, affecting focus and engagement. The ideal temperature range for most people is between 68 and 73 degrees Fahrenheit, a range that supports both comfort and effective communication.[2] Often, we overlook the importance of asking if the person we're speaking with feels comfortable with the room temperature. This small act of consideration demonstrates empathy and gives them a sense of control.

Can you remember a time when you were extremely hot or cold during an important interaction? Your ability to concentrate likely suffered as discomfort took precedence over the conversation. I've often shown videos of interviews where people noticed a suspect crossing their arms and assumed it indicated deception or stress. In reality, the room was simply cold, and the suspect was trying to stay warm. In high-stakes communications, eliminating variables that could impact comfort and attention is crucial.

Room Lighting

Proper lighting is crucial for creating a conducive environment for interaction. Natural light is preferable, as it can enhance mood and alertness. If natural light is unavailable, a combination of ambient and task lighting can create a well-lit and comfortable space. Avoid harsh fluorescent lighting, which can be glaring and uncomfortable.[3]

Proximity to the Other Person

Proxemics, the study of personal space in communication, helps determine comfort and effectiveness in interactions. The optimal distance varies based on cultural norms, relationships, and context, with general guidelines established by anthropologist Edward T. Hall. When considering proxemics in seated communication, the focus is on the upper body, which is critical to interpreting facial expressions, gestures, and posture.

Proxemic Zones:

1. **Intimate Distance (0 to 18 inches):** This distance is reserved for close relationships involving physical touch and personal communication.
2. **Personal Distance (18 inches to 4 feet):** This distance is ideal for casual conversations between friends, acquaintances, or colleagues, balancing intimacy with comfort.
3. **Social Distance (4 to 12 feet):** Suitable for formal interactions in professional or business settings, maintaining formality and respect.
4. **Public Distance (12 feet and beyond):** This distance is used for public speaking or addressing groups, minimizing personal interaction.[4]

In most interpersonal communications, I tend to position myself at the outer edge of personal distance or the closer end of social distance, typically around four feet away. During the interaction, I adjust my distance based on the situation. A chair with wheels provides the flexibility to make these adjustments smoothly if seated. This range allows for intimacy and privacy, facilitating effective communication without raising my voice while keeping a comfortable distance. Lowering your speaking volume slightly can create a sense of privacy, even at a social distance.

Conversely, you may maintain the appropriate social distance but speak too loudly or engage in excessive or intense eye contact, which can give the impression of being closer to the other person than you are.

When you invade someone's personal space, you risk making them uncomfortable and you lose the chance to observe how they might naturally show receptivity to you. For instance, when given enough space, they might move closer or remove a barrier like a purse or jacket—subtle signals that suggest good rapport or openness to your message. However, if you violate that space, you may not notice these cues—not because they aren't receptive, but because you didn't give them the opportunity to demonstrate it.

It is important to note that the perception of personal space varies significantly across cultures. In Western cultures, there is a general preference for more personal space. However, Latin America, the Middle East, and Southern European cultures will often be more comfortable being slightly closer during interactions.

THE ROLE OF PRIVACY IN DISCLOSURE

Ensuring the privacy of a conversation space is crucial for eliciting honest and open disclosure. Certain professionals, such as priests, therapists, and doctors, prioritize confidentiality and nonjudgmental environments to facilitate meaningful interactions with clients or patients.

In the Catholic tradition, individuals confess their sins in the privacy of a confessional to receive absolution. The sanctity of this confidential setting allows them to speak openly and honestly, free from fear of judgment or exposure. This environment fosters a genuine and unguarded exchange of information.

Similarly, therapists and doctors maintain private consultation rooms to protect patient confidentiality and encourage candid communication. The research underscores that the perceived privacy of the interaction space significantly influences the depth of disclosure. Patients are more likely to share sensitive information when they feel their conversations are private and secure.[5] Imagine if these interactions were conducted in public or if eavesdropping were possible—this would undoubtedly deter individuals from disclosing personal information. The assurance of confidentiality fosters trust and enhances the quality of communication between professionals and their clients or patients.[6]

Therefore, when aiming for confidential and productive conversations, it is essential to choose a private setting. A perfect environment minimizes distractions and assures participants that their disclosures will remain confidential, thus promoting openness and facilitating effective communication.

While assigned to the Chicago office, my partners and I frequently assisted a small suburban police department. We quickly discovered that their interview room setup was remarkably effective. The room featured wood paneling and carpeted floors, creating a warm, inviting atmosphere that starkly contrasted with a typical sterile police interrogation room that most people visualize. This design made individuals feel like they were conversing in a cozy, familiar setting—like sitting in their grandmother's living room.

On the other end of the spectrum, there was another police department where my partners and I conducted a ton of polygraph examinations, but it was not the ideal setup. It had a table bolted to the floor with a large brass ring for a suspect's handcuffs to be affixed and torn carpeting with dim lighting and a stale cigarette smell. On one occasion, we even noticed blood smeared on the cinder block walls. This was not a room set up to calm an individual's anxiety.

While creating a comfortable atmosphere is essential, ensuring privacy is paramount, especially when discussing deeply personal issues that the individual may not have disclosed even to their family. Conducting such sensitive conversations within potential earshot of family members can be a significant hindrance, as it may inhibit the individual from speaking openly and honestly.

Environmental factors play a significant role in influencing communication dynamics. A well-designed environment can enhance comfort, reduce anxiety, and promote openness, leading to more effective interactions. A calming environment can significantly reduce anxiety levels, making participants more receptive to communication. Elements such as soothing colors, comfortable furniture, and pleasant scents can create a relaxing atmosphere that encourages open dialogue.[7] Comfortable seating and an ergonomic setup can significantly affect participants' feelings during the interaction. Providing options for adjusting the seating arrangement can help accommodate individual preferences and enhance overall comfort.[8]

FREE OF BARRIERS

Physical barriers, such as large office desks, conference room tables, or other obstructions, can significantly hinder communication by creating a sense of separation and formality between individuals. These barriers can make interactions feel more adversarial or distant, which may prevent open, honest, and collaborative dialogue. Understanding the role of the physical environment in communication is essential for creating settings that foster positive and productive interactions.

One effective way to minimize these barriers is by choosing informal seating arrangements that naturally encourage a more collaborative and relaxed atmosphere. For example, the seating areas often found in large hotels offer an ideal environment for meaningful conversations. These spaces typically feature small clusters of chairs around low tables, creating an inviting and intimate setting. Unlike traditional office setups, where a large desk might act as a barrier between participants, these hotel seating areas are designed to reduce the physical and psychological distance between people.

The low tables in these settings are particularly beneficial because they do not obstruct the view or create a sense of division. This lack of a significant barrier allows individuals to feel more connected and engaged with each other. Moreover, the chairs in these spaces are often arranged at slight angles rather than directly facing each other. This angled positioning is crucial as it subtly shifts the interaction from a confrontational dynamic, which might occur when people sit directly opposite one another, to a more cooperative and collaborative stance. The visual cue created by this arrangement gives the impression that both parties are working together on a common goal rather than opposing one another in a direct face-to-face confrontation.

These seating arrangements are not just about comfort but also about strategically enhancing communication dynamics. The absence of large, imposing furniture and the thoughtful placement of chairs contribute to a more egalitarian interaction where both parties are encouraged to participate equally. This setup can lead to more open, honest, and effective communication, as the physical environment reinforces a sense of partnership and shared purpose. Environments free of physical barriers promote closer interpersonal distances, which can enhance the quality of communication by fostering a sense of trust and cooperation.

Furthermore, research on personal space violations highlights how removing physical barriers can reduce defensive behaviors and lead to more positive evaluations of the interaction and the people involved.[9] By reducing physical obstacles and carefully considering the seating orientation, we can create environments that encourage open dialogue, mutual understanding, and productive interactions.

An often overlooked yet crucial element of room setup is the quality of seating. A chair that's too high, too low, or plain uncomfortable can quickly disrupt focus, prompting frequent shifting that may be wrongly interpreted as nervousness or discomfort. Unfortunately, due to budget constraints, high-quality chairs are often neglected in both corporate and law enforcement settings. Interview rooms are frequently furnished with chairs that are decades old—outdated, threadbare relics passed down through the years.

I once learned this lesson the hard way. I sat down in an old, worn-out office chair during an interview. As I leaned back, the chair buckled beneath me, flipping over in a dramatic collapse that left me sprawled upside down on the floor. Regaining my composure, I found another chair in the hallway and resumed the interview, though the suspect's perception of my professionalism may have taken a noticeable hit.

A comfortable, adjustable chair is more than a piece of furniture—it's a strategic tool. The ability to subtly adjust my seat height allows me to position myself slightly higher than the person I'm speaking with, maintaining a sense of authority without appearing domineering. When you and the person you're speaking with have comfortable, supportive chairs, it creates a space where attention remains on the conversation, not on the need to shift, fidget, or adjust. In these settings, a well-chosen chair becomes an invisible ally, ensuring that every movement supports, rather than disrupts, the flow of communication. Spending a little bit of money on a quality chair can have a dramatic return on investment.

THE RIGHT EAR ADVANTAGE

Research illustrates the advantage of speaking into someone's right ear, often called the "right ear advantage" in verbal information processing, adding another layer of consideration to choosing the best location for an interaction. The right ear sends auditory signals to the brain's left hemisphere, which is more adept at handling language and verbal tasks for most individuals. As a result, auditory information received by the right ear is processed more swiftly and accurately. Studies support this advantage in processing linguistic information, demonstrating that people respond more accurately to spoken instructions delivered to their right ear.[10, 11]

In practical terms, directing crucial information to a person's right ear can enhance comprehension and efficiency in noisy environments. This right ear superiority in processing verbal communication holds true across diverse cultures, indicating a universal basis for this phenomenon. When sitting across from someone in an interview setting, I will typically try to set up the room so that I am positioned slightly off their right ear. We never want to be directly across from the person we speak to because this can be viewed as adversarial. I am creating a clamshell effect by aligning my left knee with the subject's right knee. Imagine you are conversing with someone while sitting around a campfire, and you are seated to the subject's right. In doing so, we gain body language and auditory advantage.

CHOOSING THE RIGHT MESSENGER

When preparing for any interaction—whether it's an interview, a difficult conversation, or a high-stakes negotiation—you must remember that you are part of the environment. The dynamic you bring into the room matters. Sometimes, the most effective move is to step back and ask yourself, "Am I the right person for this?" Not out of a lack of confidence but as a strategic assessment of whether someone else with a different presence or background might be better positioned to build trust and gather information in these situations.

There were instances post-9/11 where female interrogators faced unique challenges in obtaining confessions from detainees, particularly in environments with cultural or religious norms that might view women in positions of authority differently. Some detainees from conservative backgrounds, particularly from regions with strict gender roles, might have been less cooperative or willing to engage with female agents. This could sometimes impact the dynamics of the interaction. However, as in all aspects of communication effectiveness, these issues are vastly overestimated. Typically, someone's skill, approach, and tenacity bear much more weight on the outcome than their background.

Lena Sisco, a former Naval Intelligence Officer, has emphasized how female interrogators can leverage their perceived nonthreatening demeanor to establish rapport and extract vital information. Her approach contrasted sharply with the imposing presence of the Marine guards who escorted prisoners to her. Sisco's success in elicitation and interrogations highlights the critical role of empathy, cultural sensitivity, and adaptability. Her experiences demonstrate that effective communication, regardless of gender, hinges on connecting with detainees and utilizing tactical empathy to navigate cultural differences.[12]

When working with a partner, it's often beneficial to recognize who the subject is naturally gravitating toward, as this can significantly influence the dynamics of the interaction. Sometimes, individuals build rapport more easily with one person over another, which can be reflected in subtle nonverbal cues. For example, they may orient their body toward the person they feel connected to—leaning slightly in their direction or pointing their feet toward them. Conversely, they might use objects, like a purse or jacket, to create a barrier between themselves and someone they are less comfortable with.

Earlier in my career, I was called in to assist in an interview with a corporate executive who had been using his position to conduct a financial crime. It was a high-profile investigation, and my mentor Jim was the Special Agent in Charge who had requested I travel to his district to work on the case. I felt honored to be asked to work on the case but also intimidated because I was a junior agent, and it was under the spotlight of my mentor. I prepared for the case extensively. I dressed in a suit and tie, understanding the suspect was a senior executive and would also be wearing a suit and tie. I had a good background on the subject before the interaction.

During the interview before the polygraph, I asked about the subject's family, education, employment, and leisure activities. I understood his potential motives for committing a financial crime. The subject ended up failing the polygraph regarding committing the financial crime for which he was accused. I spoke with the suspect for about three hours and felt I was doing everything possible to get him to disclose his involvement in the crime. At that point, he asked me, "What's next?" This was an interesting statement. He was not saying, "I didn't do it." It was a matter-of-fact statement. I knew then that the room's power dynamic was skewed in his favor. He was a senior executive, and I was a young agent. What this man needed was someone who was on his level. The Special Agent in Charge, Jim, was that man. We would affectionally call him Yoda as he was our instructor at the federal polygraph school and had been one of the most renowned interrogators in the federal government. At this point, I couldn't have an ego. As much as I wanted to obtain a confession, the mission was more important. I walked, hat in hand, down the hallway to Jim's corner office and apprised him of the situation. I told him I did what I could, but he needed Yoda. He needed a fellow gray-haired executive who would speak plainly to him.

At this point, Jim agreed, walked down the hall, and had the following conversation with a fellow senior executive:

"Bob, I talked with Brad. He is the one I hand-picked to fly in and resolve this issue. Brad told me two things. You failed the polygraph and asked, 'What's next?' Bob, you have control over what's next. Option one, despite all three of us knowing your involvement, you choose to tell us we are wrong in our assessment. Bob, this is a busy election year, and I would rather have my agents work on protective advances and threat cases. However, I oversee this district, and if forced to do so, I will have my agents find every single dollar of fraud you are responsible for. Then, when the US attorney asks if you cooperated and accepted responsibility, I will be forced to say no. Option two, we all agree that you have had a lot of terrible things come your way over the past couple of years that have caused financial strain. It started as a loan you intended to repay, but the economic pressure increased, and you went down the rabbit hole. You are a good man who made a mistake. If that is what we are talking about, this being a mistake, let's take option two and move on."

The suspect immediately put his head down and admitted to his crimes. I was not the right person at the right time to get that disclosure. I learned that, sometimes, you must leave your ego at the door to accomplish the mission.

THE RIGHT TIME

"The early bird catches the worm, but
the second mouse gets the cheese."
—Willie Nelson

Understanding when to have a difficult conversation is as crucial as the content of the conversation itself. Our emotional and physiological states can significantly impact our decision-making abilities. Factors such as hunger, fatigue, and overall mood can influence the decisions of even the most experienced professionals. This chapter explores how these factors affect decision-making and provides practical advice on timing critical conversations to achieve the best outcomes.

The importance of conversation timing traces back to ancient Greece, where philosophers like Aristotle introduced the concept of **kairos**. This principle emphasizes that the timing of your words is just as crucial as their content. Kairos focuses on identifying the right moment to act, whether you're making a strategic decision, addressing an audience, or having a one-on-one conversation.

The Yerkes-Dodson Principle: How Stress and Pressure Impact Performance

The Yerkes-Dodson law, which states the relationship between arousal levels and performance, is crucial when considering the timing of discussions, particularly concerning the other person's psychological state. This law states that an optimal level of arousal enhances performance, though this optimal level varies depending on the task's complexity and the individual's emotional condition.

When planning a discussion, negotiation, or interview, assessing the person's current state of mind is essential, as it can significantly influence their ability to engage effectively. If an individual is under high stress or anxiety, their arousal level may be excessively high. Such heightened arousal can impair their cognitive functions, hindering clear thinking, information processing, and thoughtful responses. Their ability to process information logically in these situations is diminished. As a result, it may be beneficial to postpone the conversation until the individual is in a calmer state, where their performance and communication would be more optimal.[13]

On the other hand, if the individual is too relaxed or disengaged, their arousal level might be too low, leading to a lack of focus or motivation during the discussion. In these cases, selecting a time when they are more alert and attentive might be advantageous, ensuring they can fully participate and provide more meaningful responses. The sweet spot is finding the right time when the other party is alert but not overly emotional or stressed.

But alertness and emotional balance don't exist in a vacuum—they're heavily influenced by physiological needs. Even the most well-timed conversation can go sideways if the person is running on an empty stomach or hasn't slept well. Hunger and fatigue are two of the most common and underestimated factors that interfere with a person's ability to think clearly, regulate emotions, and engage meaningfully.

The Effects of Hunger and Fatigue

Hunger and exhaustion don't just affect mood—they directly impact cognitive function, decision-making, and self-control. Studies show that low glucose levels reduce patience, increase impulsivity, and impair complex reasoning. A hungry person is more likely to be irritable, reactive, and prone to snap judgments—hardly an ideal state for productive conversation.

Fatigue, on the other hand, disrupts risk assessment and logical thinking. Sleep-deprived individuals often swing between reckless risk-taking and overly cautious defensiveness, leading to erratic decision-making. Whether in a courtroom, a negotiation, or a difficult conversation, the physiological state of the person you're speaking with matters more than you think.

TIMING CONVERSATIONS

Consider the context in which the conversation takes place. For example, discussing a sensitive topic right before a significant event or deadline might not be ideal, and choosing a time when there are fewer external pressures can lead to better outcomes.

When I was working on child exploitation cases in Missouri, their Internet Crimes Against Children (ICAC) task force put much thought into when to conduct search warrants. They would typically not want to perform these search warrants in the morning for several reasons. First, the subjects might be sleeping, and when you conduct a search warrant during this time frame, it may cause them to grab a firearm to defend themselves before they realize it is the police. Also, after they are placed in custody, they may still be lethargic from having been sleeping, and this poses an issue with compliance and memory. Lastly, their spouse and children would often be present, making them more apprehensive about disclosing criminal conduct.

The task force did an excellent job of surveilling the house to determine the best time to conduct the search warrant. Typically, this would be when the spouse and children were not present. If they were present, they would immediately try to get the suspect to move to a tinted-out vehicle outside the house. This created a mobile "confessional" where the subject could disclose his criminal behavior and not have his family hear.

Here are some practical tips for timing conversations.

Avoid Early Mornings and Late Afternoons. The first hour of the workday isn't ideal for critical discussions—people are still transitioning from sleep and may not be fully alert. Similarly, fatigue sets in during late afternoons, making it a poor time for high-stakes interactions. Aim for midmorning or midafternoon when possible.

Schedule Conversations After Meals. If a discussion is important, time it after a meal. Research shows that higher glucose levels improve cognitive function and mood, leading to better decision-making and greater receptiveness.

Offer Refreshments. Providing snacks or beverages before a conversation can be an easy rapport-building tool. Even if the offer is declined, it activates the principle of reciprocity, making the person more inclined to engage. Additionally, caffeine and calories help stabilize energy levels, reducing irritability and enhancing focus.

I've seen this principle play out firsthand in high-stakes interrogations. Before a sensitive interview, I always offer the subject a snack and a drink. Not only does this prevent the effects of hunger from interfering, but it also subtly builds rapport—creating a dynamic where the other person is more receptive and engaged.

Even in routine cases, my partner and I made it a point to stop at local all-day breakfast diners before conducting interviews. This simple ritual ensured we were well-nourished, focused, and ready to perform at our best. By understanding and leveraging the impact of hunger and fatigue, you can ensure that conversations happen at the right time, in the right conditions, and with the best possible outcome.

By controlling where and when an interaction happens, we can dramatically improve our chances of success. The right setting creates comfort, and the right timing ensures rational decision-making. But even when conditions are optimal, one thing can still sabotage the conversation—anxiety. In the next chapter, we'll explore how to manage nervousness, build confidence, and maintain control in high-stakes situations.

CHAPTER 9

Preparing for and Weathering the Storm

"A smooth sea never made a skilled sailor."
—Franklin D. Roosevelt

The true test of any communicator is not how well they perform when everything goes according to plan, but how they navigate the unexpected—when tensions rise, nerves kick in, and uncertainty takes over. No matter how much preparation goes into an important conversation, anxiety can still creep in. A racing heart, dry mouth, rapid speech—these are all physiological responses designed to protect us, but ones that can just as easily hinder us in high-stakes interactions. I know this feeling well.

During my first solo polygraph on a double homicide case, anxiety took hold just when I needed to be composed the most. The moment I began confronting the suspect with the polygraph results, my voice betrayed me—pitch rising, pace quickening. In seconds, I lost control of the room. The suspect sensed my nerves, asked for a lawyer, and shut down completely.

I left that room frustrated—not just because I had lost the interaction but because I hadn't anticipated how my own physiology would react under pressure. That day, I realized something crucial: It wasn't just about knowing what to say. It was about preparing myself mentally and physically to express it with confidence.

This chapter will explore how to anticipate, manage, and overcome the inevitable waves of anxiety that arise in critical conversations. We'll cover practical strategies to prepare for high-pressure situations, techniques to maintain composure when emotions run high, and methods to ensure that when the moment of truth arrives, you're in complete control of your own response.

TECHNIQUES FOR LOWERING ANXIETY

Performance anxiety is common in presentations, job interviews, and other significant events. Fortunately, several techniques can help lower anxiety levels before a performance.

Preparation

A study examined the impact of preparation on anxiety in high-stakes environments, explicitly focusing on NFL quarterbacks and Secret Service Agents. The research revealed that extensive preparation significantly reduced anxiety levels for individuals in both fields. For NFL quarterbacks, comprehensive playbook knowledge allowed them to anticipate player positions without visual cues, helping them navigate unexpected situations more effectively during games. This preparation instilled a sense of control and confidence, enabling them to adapt and improvise under pressure.[1]

Similarly, Secret Service Agents who meticulously prepared for protective events experienced reduced anxiety. From my personal experience, organizing a protection detail for high-level dignitaries can be overwhelming. However, detailed knowledge of the environment—such as the layout of a hotel, the function of each door, and the roles of all personnel—provides agents with a critical sense of control. This mirrors how NFL quarterbacks script the first few plays of a game, allowing them to rehearse mentally until actions become second nature. Such preparation builds confidence and brings physiological benefits, such as lower resting heart rates and improved resilience to stress, making individuals better equipped to handle high-pressure and physical situations.

Prior to high-stakes interviews, I prepare by visualizing each phase of the interaction—the handshake, the opening questions, potential objections, and, most importantly, a successful conclusion. This mental preparation allows me to foresee challenges and refine my responses, enhancing my adaptability in the moment.

Before every performance, the U.S. Navy's Blue Angels engage in a precise visualization ritual. They sit together, eyes closed, and "fly" the entire routine in their minds—calling out commands, mimicking movements, and visualizing each stunt down to the smallest detail. This technique, often called "chair flying," taps into the brain's powerful ability to simulate real experiences through mental imagery. This visualization activates the same brain regions as actual movement, effectively rehearsing the act without ever leaving the ground. The result? Sharper focus, reduced anxiety, and flawless execution when it counts most. Whether you're preparing for a flight show or a tough conversation, the principle is the same: Mental reps matter.

In the military, Red Team exercises are crucial for preparation. They simulate adversarial forces, enabling teams to identify weaknesses, uncover strategic flaws, and enhance their tactics before execution. A notable example is the Navy SEAL mission to eliminate Osama bin Laden, where the team rehearsed in a full-scale replica of his compound. This realistic training helped them refine their strategies and develop the composure needed to execute flawlessly under pressure. It also allowed them to practice scenarios that deviated from the plan, such as the loss of a helicopter during insertion. This preparatory work certainly supported the team's swift and composed response during the actual event.

Become Comfortable Being Uncomfortable

A key realization I've had—both on the Brazilian Jiu-Jitsu mats and in conversation—is that real growth starts when comfort ends. In BJJ, I often begin training rounds from less favorable positions where my opponent has a notable advantage or is about to attempt a submission. This approach is crucial; it keeps me calm under pressure, allows me to manage my breathing, and enables me to think clearly in threatening situations. If I can stay composed in those challenging moments, I can do the same anywhere.

The same principle holds for effective communication. Practicing only in favorable circumstances equates to hoping rather than preparing. True preparation involves intentionally simulating adversity: What if your microphone malfunctions? What if you trip over your words during your introduction? What if you make a bad first impression? Don't merely picture success—train for challenges. Develop mental scripts and recovery tactics. Practice responding gracefully, re-engaging your audience, and restoring rapport after a misstep.

This principle is foundational in expert training across varied fields: Top performers prepare not just for what should go right but for what might go wrong. They also deconstruct complex performances into manageable parts—a strategy called chunking—mastering each component under stress before merging them into a cohesive whole.[2] This strategy is akin to what elite chess instructors employ by starting students with endgame situations instead of full-board openings. Presenting novices with all 32 pieces can be intimidating. However, by placing them in a focused scenario—with just a king, several pawns, and a clear goal—they can recognize patterns, leverage strategy, and build genuine confidence.

I apply this same method when teaching polygraph techniques and interview preparation. Instead of rehearsing entire conversations from start to finish, we segment interactions into critical parts—the introduction, a brief overview, and navigating the subject's Miranda warnings. By isolating these emotional and tactical hurdles, students cultivate the confidence and muscle memory necessary for effective performance under pressure.

The same concept applies in business. Salespeople, negotiators, and presenters often feel burdened by the breadth of their responsibilities. However, by chunking their preparation into vital components—like delivering an engaging opening, handling objections smoothly, or responding to surprising resistance—they can prepare effectively. Visualization also plays a crucial role—not as passive daydreaming, but as active rehearsal. By frequently visualizing successful outcomes in high-stakes, awkward situations, you train your mind and body to recognize these scenarios as familiar. When the moment arrives, you will act as if you have encountered it before.

The following examples demonstrate how scenario-based training can improve preparation and lessen anxiety in high-pressure contexts:

Sales

- Objection Management: Practice responding to common objections ("too expensive," "happy with my current provider") until your reactions feel instinctive and assured.
- Elevator Pitch: Rehearse delivering a captivating 60-second value statement spontaneously.

Negotiations

- Responding to Unexpected Questions: Practice maintaining composure while addressing surprising, emotional, or unrelated queries.
- Negotiating Without Notes: Simulate negotiations without notes or slides; focus on conveying essential points from memory.

Presentations

- Technology Failure Exercise: Rehearse the full presentation without visual aids to increase engagement through vocal delivery, pacing, and presence.
- Q&A Challenge: Have peers act as a critical or skeptical audi ence during Q&A; practice providing clear, composed responses.

The top communicators—much like elite athletes, pilots, and special forces members—don't just prepare for success; they rehearse for adversity. They consciously engage in uncomfortable scenarios, dissect complex interactions into pivotal moments, and master each aspect before bringing everything together. They visualize, simulate, and rehearse—not to abolish anxiety altogether, but to ensure they have the knowledge to navigate challenges when they arise.

Nevertheless, no level of preparation can completely suppress the body's instinctual stress response. Therefore, learning to manage your physiological reactions in real time is the next vital step in becoming ready.

Breathing Exercises

Breathing exercises are widely recognized for their efficacy in lowering anxiety and promoting relaxation. They engage the body's parasympathetic nervous system, triggering a "rest and digest" response that counteracts the stress-inducing effects of the sympathetic nervous system. This state reduces stress levels, blood pressure, and resting heart rate, making individuals more efficient at detecting deception during interactions.[3] Additionally, it allows better regulation of the amygdala, preventing overly emotional responses during the interview.

Before beginning an interaction, I habitually spend two minutes doing a quick 4/7/8 breathing exercise. I close the door to my interview room, sit comfortably, and breathe deeply through my nose, allowing my stomach to expand for four seconds. I then hold my breath for seven seconds. Lastly, I slowly exhale through my mouth for eight seconds. I can use the heart rate monitor on my watch and see it drop noticeably.

Physical Fitness

Maintaining optimal physical condition is crucial for reducing anxiety. Regular physical fitness activities, such as aerobic exercise or strength training, release endorphins and reduce stress levels. Physical fitness enhances sleep quality, positively influencing mental clarity and cognitive function. Furthermore, a lower resting heart rate resulting from regular exercise indicates an enhanced ability to manage stressors before they escalate into anxiety.

Being in good physical condition offers additional benefits, such as improving one's ability to detect deception. A recent study has shown that resting heart rate significantly predicts one's ability to distinguish between truthful and deceptive statements. Specifically, individuals with a lower resting heart rate were better at detecting lies. The study suggests that it might be associated with lower physiological arousal, which could enhance cognitive performance and attention to detail. This enhanced cognitive performance may help individuals better discern subtle cues indicative of deception.[4]

Upon my graduation from polygraph school, my partners introduced me to a CrossFit-style workout regimen. This high-intensity fitness program combines weight lifting, cardio, and body weight exercises. The focus was on varied functional movements performed at high intensity to improve overall fitness. I believe the commitment to physical fitness played a role in our ability to perform at a high level in the interview room. It increases our physical and cognitive endurance during lengthy interactions. It allows us to regulate the initial physiological rush better, which sometimes takes place when we are engaging in sensitive conversations.

Improvisation

The qualities that make a good quarterback—preparation, poise, and confidence—parallel those that make a good communicator. Notably, figures like Patrick Mahomes or Peyton Manning exemplify the ability to be audible and creative when the playbook falls short, underscoring the importance of adaptability in communication.

One of the most important influences on my development as an effective communicator was my involvement in improvisational acting. I began competing in improv during high school and continued pursuing it into college. As I came to understand that I was more introverted by nature, improv became both a challenge and a catalyst for growth. It pushed me to step out of my comfort zone and develop the confidence to engage with others in real time. The ability to think quickly, adapt on the spot, and access the creative right side of the brain became invaluable—not just onstage, but in everyday conversations. One of the most popular forms of improv, for instance, involves performers responding to unpredictable scenarios with no script, relying solely on instinct, timing, and teamwork—all essential tools for effective communication.

While serving eight years as an instructor at the National Center for Credibility Assessment, I encouraged my trainees to incorporate improvisation principles into their practical exercises. This facility, situated at Fort Jackson, South Carolina, trains personnel from federal law enforcement and intelligence agencies to become polygraph examiners. We conducted mock interviews involving United States Army Basic Training Course recruits. In these scenarios, I challenged my trainees to insert random words, song lyrics, and movie quotes into their interactions with the recruits.

While many initially questioned the purpose of such exercises and feared failure, the people I trained who embraced these techniques soon recognized the value of being adaptable and breaking free from having a rigid mindset. This "improvisation" sometimes allowed them to enter a flow state during the interaction. It fostered confidence and forced the trainees to break free of their typical mindsets and communication strategies.

In one instance, I asked one of my trainees, an FBI agent, to subtly incorporate several specific words into her mock crime scenario with a basic training recruit. Before the interview, I informed the soldiers that the FBI agent would attempt to sneak these words into the conversation and challenged them to detect the insertion. The agent was highly skilled but tended to be rigid in her approach, so I gave her multiple random words to help her develop more flexibility. The challenging words included "Burkina Faso," "salve," "General Shalikashvili," "Madagascar aye-aye lemur," and "Medal of Valor."

When I assigned this task, I thought it would be impossible for the agent to seamlessly integrate such a selection of words into the discussion without being detected. However, I was amazed by her creativity. She introduced herself to the recruit and said, "I know you met Special Agent Beeler already. I don't know if he told you, but he's famous. He just returned from Burkina Faso, where he was on a security detail for General Shalikashvili. Remarkably, a rare Madagascar aye-aye lemur crossed in front of their limo at high speed, but he managed to avoid it. Unfortunately, a follow-up vehicle in the motorcade clipped the animal. The local authorities were devastated since it was one of the last breeding pairs of this endangered species. Agent Beeler skillfully used his medical training to apply an antiseptic salve to its wounds, and the lemur survived. He was awarded the Medal of Valor for his actions."

I was in awe of how skillfully and convincingly the agent delivered this story. Both of us were surprised when the soldier immediately responded, "Oh yeah, I heard about that." The agent then continued with the interview, which was the best I had witnessed her conduct during the three-month training program.

Imitation

The saying "Imitation is the ultimate form of flattery" perfectly captures the essence of learning new skills. I firmly believe that the best way to master new knowledge is by observing experts in the field. Brazilian Jiu-Jitsu is a prime example. Years ago, learning was confined to your local professor, which could be limiting if they didn't provide the insights needed to realize your full potential. However, platforms like YouTube and TikTok have revolutionized this by offering access to thousands of instructors worldwide, each presenting diverse perspectives and techniques. Even with access to one of the world's best instructors, I have significantly benefited from visiting other Brazilian Jiu-Jitsu schools and experiencing various teaching styles.

The influence of imitation is notably demonstrated in the evolution of gameplay in the video game *Tetris*. Originally invented in 1984, achieving a perfect score was a rare feat not accomplished until 2009. However, since then, perfect scores have become a daily occurrence. This shift is attributed to the availability of online resources, such as YouTube, where players can watch others mastering the game and then replicate their techniques. This phenomenon underscores how access to shared knowledge and imitation can rapidly accelerate skill development in gaming and other areas.[5]

In my teaching role at the National Center for Credibility Assessment, I was fortunate to be an instructor to trainees representing the 31 federal intelligence and law enforcement agencies that utilized the program. Initially, I would show them some of my previous interviews. This would serve as a stock template as they learned to enhance their communication skills. However, I did not want them to become a version of me. I wanted them to become the best version of themselves. Providing them with a communication starter kit they could imitate in their initial stages of development was very beneficial.

Beta-Blockers

I want to preface my discussion about beta-blockers by stating that I am not a doctor and do not provide medical advice. However, their use for treating performance anxiety, particularly in public speaking or performing, is well-documented.

Beta-blockers work by suppressing the effects of the hormone epinephrine (adrenaline), which is responsible for the fight-or-flight response. This response can manifest as an increased heart rate, rapid breathing, and excessive sweating, which can negatively impact performance. When taken under a doctor's care, prescription beta-blockers can reduce heart rate, blood pressure, and sweating before and during high-stakes interactions.

Several studies have demonstrated the effectiveness of beta-blockers in performance settings. For instance, research published in the *American Journal of Psychiatry* found that beta-blockers significantly reduced anxiety symptoms in musicians during performances. By lowering the impact of adrenaline and shutting down the negative feedback loop of its effects on an individual's physiology, beta-blockers can enhance their confidence heading into and throughout a high-stakes interaction.[6]

WEATHER THE STORM WITH COMPOSURE

"The battlefield is a scene of constant chaos.
The winner will be the one who controls that
chaos, both his own and the enemy's."
—Napoleon Bonaparte

In my line of work, I regularly engage with some of the most reprehensible individuals on the planet—murderers, rapists, and child molesters. These individuals frequently attempt to provoke an emotional reaction from me, hoping to gain the upper hand. The rest of this chapter will explore methods for creating and maintaining emotional control during sensitive communications.

Allowing emotions to dictate our responses makes us vulnerable to manipulation. Emotional reactions can cloud judgment, impair decision-making, and lead to unfavorable outcomes. In contrast, maintaining a calm demeanor enables us to think clearly, stay focused on our objectives, and manage the conversation more effectively.

This is easier said than done. When someone makes a provocative or insensitive statement, I try to pause and avoid reflexively responding. Taking a deep breath—without sighing in a way that could be perceived as disdain or contempt—helps in this process. Focusing on the objective reminds me that becoming emotional could cause the subject to terminate the interaction. I concentrate on the bigger picture of what I am trying to accomplish. I might need to bite my tongue in the short term, but achieving my goal signifies a successful outcome.

The Role of Empathy and Emotional Detachment

When interacting with individuals accused of heinous crimes, it is essential to see things from their perspective to establish and maintain rapport. I often adopt a role like that of their publicist or defense counsel, blaming the situation for their choices, understanding their actions, and diminishing the impact of their behavior. This empathetic approach creates an environment where they feel more comfortable opening up about their transgressions.

Controlling emotions is crucial in these situations. Taking things personally can quickly escalate into arguments, with both parties becoming entrenched and defensive. I frequently reference Viktor Frankl, a renowned psychiatrist and Holocaust survivor, when discussing emotional control. In his book *Man's Search for Meaning*, Frankl explores how he mentally survived the concentration camps. One of his quotes profoundly resonates with me: "Between stimulus and response, there is a space. In that space, we have the power to choose our response. In our response lies our growth and our freedom."[7] This statement from a man who endured unimaginable suffering underscores the importance of controlling our responses to external stimuli.

This philosophy is particularly relevant when dealing with individuals who have committed serious crimes, such as child molestation or murder. Despite the natural inclination to express my true feelings toward them, I must harness the space between stimulus and response to control primal emotions and remain professional. This emotional detachment is vital for achieving the mission's goals.

In some situations, immediate reactions are necessary, such as in our protective mission, where the team closest to the principal protectee must act swiftly in the face of a threat, prioritizing safety over deliberation. However, we have the luxury of time in most scenarios, especially during conversations. We can choose to respond thoughtfully rather than react impulsively.

Taking a moment to reflect allows us to avoid knee-jerk reactions and respond calmly, reasonably, and constructively. This approach is particularly valuable in high-stakes conversations, where thoughtful responses are beneficial and crucial. Measured reactions can lead to better outcomes and more positive interaction, underscoring the importance of your role in these situations.

Professionalism and Adaptability

In the Secret Service, we may hold personal political beliefs, but our responsibility is to remain nonpartisan. We are sworn to protect the office, not the individual. This duty extends beyond domestic figures; it includes safeguarding foreign heads of state, whether they are allies or adversaries of the United States. Such consistent exposure to vastly different cultures, belief systems, and political ideologies expands your worldview. It certainly expanded mine.

Over time, I learned to enter conversations not with the aim of agreement but with a clear sense of purpose. My job wasn't to convert or confront; it was to connect just long enough to build trust, uncover the truth, or prevent harm. This disciplined focus, especially in high-stakes environments, demands the ability to shift gears without losing your grounding. I had to adapt my communication style while staying anchored in my values and professional intent.

This same mindset is just as useful outside the Secret Service—in workplaces, relationships, and everyday interactions. When you're speaking with someone whose views you may not share, the goal isn't to win the exchange; it's to keep the dialogue open and constructive. One practical way to do that is by acknowledging what you observe in the other person's behavior or tone without judgment or assumption.

Instead of reacting emotionally, you might say something like, "That issue clearly carries a lot of weight for you," or "There's a lot behind what you just said." Statements like these gently reflect emotional content while signaling that you're paying attention. They create space for the other person to speak more openly.

This kind of reflective communication is a foundational skill taught in crisis negotiation programs worldwide. From hostage negotiation courses to crisis intervention models, law enforcement professionals are trained to listen deeply and acknowledge emotions—not as a tactic, but as a pathway to trust. When used genuinely, this approach helps calm emotional intensity and opens the door to reasoned conversation.[8]

By focusing on understanding instead of interruption, and on reflection rather than reaction, you strengthen emotional control and establish rapport—whether you're in an interrogation room or across the table at home.

Overcoming Preconceived Notions

Over the years, I interviewed hundreds of child molesters and murderers. These are some of the worst people that inhabit the planet. However, at the start of these interactions, I did not know if they had committed the act for which they were suspected. I could not bring any preconceived notions about the person into the equation. I needed to be genuinely interested in the person I was interacting with. They needed to feel I cared about their situation and had not already decided on their potential guilt.

Understanding Another Person's Perspective

I strongly advocate diversifying one's news sources in today's tribal culture, where individuals often find themselves in divided echo chambers. Breaking out of these ideological bubbles and seeking information from various perspectives is crucial. For instance, occasionally tuning in to MSNBC can provide a different viewpoint if someone identifies as conservative. Likewise, a liberal individual might find it valuable to watch Fox News occasionally. I prioritize news sources free from political spin or partisan commentary, leveraging the numerous applications and websites that offer unbiased reporting. This helps me navigate conversations with a diverse audience.

Case Study: Composure in a Double Homicide Interrogation

One of the most powerful displays of emotional control I've witnessed in law enforcement occurred during a double homicide interrogation I conducted with my partner Brian.

We assisted in a case where two individuals had been fatally shot inside a vehicle. The police had two suspects in custody. The first suspect, who had no prior criminal record, was believed to have been present but not the actual shooter. During our interview with him, he became very cooperative and disclosed that he was present during the shooting and told us the second suspect had thrown the murder weapon in a local canal. He also informed us that the motive for the shooting was their belief that the victims were planning to retaliate against them due to a previous altercation.

The second suspect—the alleged shooter—was an entirely different story. As soon as we entered the room, he launched into a hostile tirade. He hurled insults, cursed at us, and tried to provoke a confrontation. To someone inexperienced, it may have seemed like he was genuinely furious. However, Brian, ever composed and observant, noticed several inconsistencies revealing this was an act, not authentic rage:

- His hands weren't clenched, and he didn't move aggressively.
- His voice lacked tension—it was loud, but not strained.
- His posture was loose, not squared up or threatening.
- He escalated too quickly, shifting from neutral to enraged in seconds—classic signs of performative anger.
- He breathed evenly—no shallow breaths or flared nostrils typically observed in actual high-arousal states.

Rather than reacting defensively, Brian did something subtle but powerful: He slowed down. He softened his voice, maintained a relaxed posture, and gave the suspect nothing to bounce his aggression off. It was the conversational equivalent of redirecting a punch and allowing the attacker to stumble forward.

As the suspect's nervous energy began to taper off, Brian shifted the tone:

"I understand you were in a tough situation. I know for a fact you thought these people were going to hurt you. I also know for a fact where you threw the gun into the canal after the shooting. I don't think you're a monster; I believe you made a rash, poor decision based on emotion. Is that what we're discussing?"

That one sentence accomplished what yelling back or escalating never could. The suspect took a long breath and dropped his shoulders—an involuntary signal of emotional release. Seconds later, he confessed to pulling the trigger.

He was later convicted of double homicide and sentenced to life in prison.

This case underscores a vital truth: You don't win high-stakes conversations by overpowering your opponent—you win by mastering yourself. Emotional control is not just about staying calm; it's about creating the conditions for truth to emerge. Composure becomes a force multiplier when combined with sharp observation and tactical empathy.

Mastering composure under pressure is a crucial skill for effective communication. We've explored how to anticipate and manage anxiety, equipping ourselves to stay calm, confident, and in control during any interaction. But composure alone isn't enough—what truly matters is how we use it. In the next chapter, we'll explore the psychology of ethical influence and how to apply it to enhance communication, foster connection, and guide conversations toward better outcomes.

CHAPTER 10

How to SCORE Trust—Using Ethical Influence in Communication

"It is wise to persuade people to do things and make them think it was their own idea."
—Nelson Mandela

We've all been in conversations where trust felt natural—where someone seemed to "get us" without effort. And we've all experienced the opposite: guarded, tense exchanges where no real connection took root. What makes the difference? It's not just what we say, but how we make people feel.

Whether you're trying to gain honest insight in an interview, negotiate a sensitive issue, or simply build better rapport, one truth applies: People are more likely to trust and open up when they feel good and more likely to shut down when they feel threatened.

This chapter will show you how to influence the emotional and psychological state of others ethically by understanding what's happening beneath the surface—on a chemical level. By learning to recognize the signals of stress (cortisol) and motivation (dopamine), you'll be able to guide conversations with greater purpose, empathy, and precision.

Understanding neurochemistry is just one part of the equation. To communicate with real influence, you also need structure. This is where the SCORE framework comes into play—a practical, five-part approach designed to help you create psychological safety, build connections, and guide people toward openness and truth. Let's begin by exploring the powerful chemistry of human interaction and how mastering it can change the way people respond to you.

UNDERSTANDING THE NEUROCHEMICAL DRIVERS OF HUMAN INTERACTION

Our interactions, conversations, and decisions are profoundly influenced by two powerful neurochemicals: dopamine and cortisol. These invisible forces serve as an internal emotional thermostat, constantly guiding our actions. Mastering their interplay is key to unlocking unparalleled trust, influence, and connection.

Dopamine: The Engine of Motivation

Often misconstrued as simply the "happiness" chemical, dopamine is more accurately the driving force behind pursuit, ambition, and motivation. It propels us toward goals, desires, and rewards, igniting our passions' relentless drive.[1] Everyone has unique dopamine triggers—achievements, validations, social status, hobbies—and identifying these allows you to strategically guide conversations, fostering enthusiasm and positive engagement. Think of dopamine as the engine of human motivation, driving us toward what excites us most.[2]

Cortisol: The Built-In Alarm System

Conversely, cortisol acts as our internal alarm system, activating in response to stress, anxiety, or perceived threats. Elevated cortisol levels trigger defensive behaviors, making us guarded, suspicious, or resistant.[3] This stress response creates barriers to open communication, trust, and truthfulness. Recognizing and managing cortisol levels is crucial for building lasting connections and positively influencing others. Skilled management of these stress points allows you to calm tense situations, reassure others, and create an environment conducive to meaningful exchanges.

The Power of Neurochemical Regulation: Building Genuine Rapport

Understanding the delicate balance between dopamine and cortisol offers a significant advantage in human interactions. Elevating dopamine while reducing cortisol fosters openness, receptivity, and trust. This isn't about manipulation, but about ethical influence built on understanding human nature and neurochemistry. Recognizing and adapting to these emotional undercurrents allows you to become a powerful communicator, capable of naturally steering conversations, managing emotions, and building lasting trust.

Practical Applications: Identifying Triggers and Stressors

Everyone has passions that ignite them (dopamine triggers) and stressors that weigh them down (cortisol sources). In any interaction, the key is to identify the following in the other person or people:

- **Dopamine Triggers:** What do they crave, enjoy, or seek?
- **Cortisol Sources:** What do they fear, stress over, or avoid?

In interviews, for example, questions designed to reveal emotional drivers can be powerful:

- **Dopamine Triggers (Positive Reinforcement):**
  - "What was the best thing to happen in your life?"
  - "If you had more free time, how would you spend it?"
- **Cortisol Triggers (Stress Points):**
  - "What is the worst thing to happen in your life?"
  - "What brings you the most stress in your current life?"

These questions help shape conversations by increasing dopamine (offering incentives, validation, or curiosity) or managing cortisol (reducing pressure, providing reassurance). Adopting a calming presence, like a beekeeper pumping smoke into the hive, can be effective when cortisol is high.

By recognizing what motivates and stresses others, we can adjust our approach to foster openness, trust, and influence. However, managing neurochemistry alone isn't enough; we must also apply a structured strategy to maximize connection and persuasion.

This is where the SCORE framework comes into play. By integrating Social Proof, Curiosity, Observation, Respect, and Exchange, we create an environment where people feel psychologically safe, engaged, and willing to share. These elements work in harmony with the brain's natural responses, reinforcing trust and shaping behavior in a way that leads to more meaningful interactions. Now, let's explore how to leverage SCORE to elevate communication and influence.

S—SOCIAL PROOF: THE POWER OF THE CROWD

Solomon Asch's groundbreaking experiments in the 1950s revealed the profound influence of group pressure on individual decision-making. In a seemingly straightforward vision test, participants were asked to determine which of three lines was the longest—a task that was effortless when judged independently. However, when placed in a group setting where actors posing as fellow participants deliberately gave incorrect answers, the results shifted dramatically. Unaware of the deception, many participants conformed to the majority's incorrect responses, even when their own senses and logic told them otherwise. Approximately 75% of participants agreed with the obviously wrong answer at least once, highlighting our innate tendency to align with the group.[4]

This powerful force, also known as social proof, suggests that people look to others to determine appropriate behavior, especially in uncertain situations. The fundamental human need to belong and feel accepted profoundly shapes our choice. Key aspects of social proof include:

- **Uncertainty:** When unsure, we naturally look to others for guidance.
- **Similarity:** We trust and follow those who appear similar to us.
- **Numbers:** The more people who are behaving a certain way, the stronger the influence.

Imagine traveling in an unfamiliar town and deciding where to eat. Between two restaurants, you're likely to choose the one bustling with activity or boasting higher ratings online. The busy scene offers reassuring evidence that others have made a wise decision.

A friend of mine and former Secret Service Agent Tobias Hyman operates Hyman's Seafood in Charleston, South Carolina, alongside his father and brother. It is a historic landmark in downtown Charleston, known for its rich tradition and excellent seafood. When tourists stroll through the charming streets of Charleston and start to feel hungry, they often find themselves drawn to Hyman's Seafood. The long line outside, the enticing aroma of freshly prepared seafood, and the lively buzz of activity all serve as powerful indicators. Seeing the smiles on the faces of the guests inside the restaurant helps validate one's decision. Add in a complimentary hush puppy from the manager, and you'll be eager to put your name on the waiting list. Social proof is at work here, influencing decisions with the unspoken message that "if everyone is doing it, it must be right." In this case, the crowds are right; try the Carolina Delight—you won't regret it.

Social proof has proven invaluable in my professional experience, especially during critical investigations. For instance, I might tell someone, "I've spoken to many individuals facing similar circumstances," easing their anxiety and encouraging openness by showing they're not alone.

Case Study: Texas Homicide Investigation

A powerful example of leveraging social proof emerged from a high-stakes homicide investigation in Texas involving a missing person who was presumed deceased. The primary suspect, who had been apprehended with the victim's belongings, was visibly anxious and displayed hostility toward law enforcement. Recognizing the urgency of quickly establishing rapport, I strategically employed social proof.

Prior to interviewing the suspect, I arranged for a police department volunteer to assist. As we escorted the suspect toward the interview room, the volunteer approached me openly, warmly hugging me and expressing sincere gratitude for my respectful and compassionate manner. The suspect observed this exchange carefully, witnessing a positive interaction demonstrating my character.

This carefully orchestrated yet genuine interaction utilized social proof to subtly shape the suspect's perception of me, positioning me as empathetic and trustworthy. The underlying message was clear: Others trusted me, and perhaps he should also. Evolutionarily, humans find reassurance in conforming to social norms and behaviors others exhibit, especially in uncertain situations.

This subtle display influenced the suspect, who became notably more cooperative during questioning. He ultimately confessed to killing the elderly female and led us directly to the victim's location. This instance vividly illustrates how effectively social proof and priming can influence outcomes, especially in high-stakes, emotionally charged interactions.

Social proof lays the groundwork for influence by tapping into our innate tendency to follow the crowd, but true connection requires more than external validation—it demands genuine engagement. While people may be influenced by what others are doing, they are much more likely to open up when they feel genuinely seen and understood. This is where curiosity becomes the bridge between influence and meaningful connection. By showing sincere interest in others, you create an environment where they feel valued and heard, making them more willing to share, trust, and engage. Let's explore how *curiosity* acts as the catalyst for deeper conversations and stronger relationships.

C—CURIOSITY: THE CATALYST FOR CONNECTION

Genuine curiosity forms the foundation of any successful interaction. As Ted Lasso famously advised, "Be curious, not judgmental." This simple yet profound statement encapsulates the essence of effective communication. Judgment erects barriers, hindering genuine connection and understanding. Conversely, curiosity opens doors, fostering trust and inviting openness. Dale Carnegie's timeless advice, "Be interested to be interesting," reinforces this principle. People are far more inclined to relax and share when they sense genuine interest in their lives. This approach enriches your knowledge and boosts your likability, creating a positive feedback loop that strengthens your relationships.

To harness the power of conversational chemistry, it's essential to guide conversations strategically. Especially during initial meetings, direct the conversation toward topics that genuinely interest the other person. Ask open-ended questions like "What is it about your job that you enjoy?" or "What sparked your interest in this hobby?" These questions invite them to share their passions and experiences, triggering a dopamine release and fostering a connection.

Uncovering "Addictions" and Using Them to Steer the Conversation

While "addiction" often carries a negative connotation, let's use it here to describe something positive: a passion or interest that brings joy and fulfillment. For me, that's Brazilian Jiu-Jitsu. It calms my nerves after a long day, and the people at my gym are my tribe. By uncovering the "addictions" in others, you can gain valuable insights into their motivations and steer the conversation. In any interaction, I aim to discover this "addiction," whether they reveal it directly or I uncover it through thoughtful questions. Once I identify it, it becomes a valuable tool. I can use it to refocus the conversation, much like a laser pointer captures a cat's attention. By understanding their passion, I can guide the discussion when needed.

Uncovering Deeper Connections with "What Is It About . . . ?"

When someone talks about their hobbies or work, a simple question can unlock a deeper understanding: "What is it about . . . ?" Often, people share interests I know little about. But asking this question reveals the real reasons behind their passion. People are busy; if they *choose* to dedicate time to something, it's important to them. It's not about *my* interests, but about finding the hidden motivations, the "underside of *their* iceberg"—what's not evident at a surface-level observation. Even if I don't share their specific passion, we might find a common thread on a deeper level.

Imagine you're at a party, chatting with someone who loves fishing, a hobby you don't understand. Instead of pretending to be a fishing expert, ask, "What is it about fishing that you enjoy?"

They might surprise you. They might say it's not about catching fish at all, but about escaping into nature, enjoying peace away from the distractions of daily life. Suddenly, you realize you share a desire for tranquility and escape. You don't fish, but you love to hike, and you do it for the same reasons. This realization now opens doors to connecting at another level.

Unlocking Stories Through Ink: Tattoos as Conversation Starters

Just as "What is it about . . . ?" reveals the deeper motivations behind seemingly disparate hobbies, tattoos can serve as a window into an individual's unique story. Tattoos often hold deeply personal meanings, acting as visual narratives of significant life experiences.

I've had success using tattoos as conversation starters. Many people put deep thought into their ink, making it a window into their identity. I routinely compliment people and ask them about the background behind their tattoos. Typically, people put a lot of thought into their tattoo design and are eager to share this information, providing a window into significant moments of their lives. I have obtained traction in talking to numerous individuals about their tattoos.

In one case, a suspect was suspected of involvement in a gang shooting that led to the death of a young girl as a result of a stray bullet. During the interview, I noticed his tattoos: playing cards, a large portrait tribute of his grandmother, and the words "respect" and "force." The suspect failed the polygraph regarding his involvement in the shooting. During the follow-up interview, I used his tattoos as a bridge to connect with him and help him rationalize his actions. I lightly touched the tattoo of playing cards and remarked that life had dealt him a tough hand—both in his upbringing and in this situation. Then, pointing to the words "respect" and "force" inked on his hands, I acknowledged that sometimes people feel disrespected and respond with force. At that moment, his demeanor shifted—his eyes welled up with emotion.

Sensing the opening, I moved to the most prominent tattoo: a portrait of his grandmother on his chest. I asked, "What would she want you to do?" His response was immediate: "Tell the truth." Moments later, he admitted to firing the shots at rival gang members, tragically killing a young girl with one of the stray bullets.

Each tattoo told a story—playing cards reflected the unpredictability of his life, "respect" and "force" captured his worldview, and his grandmother's image symbolized the moral compass he still clung to.

By exploring the deeper meaning behind these symbols, I guided him toward his values, leading him to his own moment of truth. Curiosity opens doors that judgment slams shut.

Learning Through Curiosity

In my role as an interviewer, I made it a point to extract at least one piece of valuable information from every person I encountered. During my graduate studies, I participated in the Drug Use Forecasting (DUF) project, a national initiative aimed at tracking drug use trends through jail interviews with arrested individuals in large metropolitan areas. Being from a small town, I had not interacted with a diverse population of criminals in the past. I had no playbook for how I could get them to open up. Initially, many of the subjects were hesitant and guarded, understandably so. However, by adopting a curious, rather than accusatory, approach, I established a rapport that encouraged them to share their experiences. Despite the criminal charges they faced, each individual possessed a unique area of expertise, offering insights that broadened my understanding of various aspects of life.

Instead of relying on direct interrogation, open-ended questions like "Tell me about . . ." or "How do you go about . . . ?" sparked deeper conversations. This approach unveiled a broad range of skills I would never have otherwise learned—from smuggling drugs and forging prison knives to spotting undercover cops. Every day felt like a podcast titled *Learn How to Do Messed-Up Stuff.* When you ask someone how they do something, they assume the role of teacher while you become the student, which fosters respect and builds trust. Essentially, curiosity breaks down barriers that direct interrogation cannot.

You create an environment where individuals feel seen and heard through genuine curiosity. I often tell those I am training, "I don't want to be the most interesting man in the world; I want to be the most interested man in the world." Curiosity ignites engagement, while observation sharpens it. Observation connects curiosity with meaningful action, giving you the ability to recognize subtle behavioral patterns, anticipate emotions, and adjust your approach accordingly.

The Power of Curiosity in a High-Stakes Case

Fresh out of initial agent training with the Secret Service, I was assigned to the counterfeit squad at the Chicago Field Office. It was an exciting opportunity, but I was inexperienced—and I knew it. The first case I was given involved a counterfeiter causing a stir across the Midwest. In the late 1990s, counterfeiters increasingly used all-in-one printer/scanner/copiers to produce fake currency. But this individual took it one step further. He developed a technique to simulate the watermark and security thread by sandwiching tracing paper images between two thin sheets of paper. While not perfect, it was clever and effective enough to fool most cashiers who relied on a counterfeit detection pen or looking for the watermark in the bill.

During interviews with suspects arrested with his counterfeit bills, I learned the man behind the operation called himself "Art." He claimed to be the world's best counterfeiter but no one I talked to knew his full name. They described a tall, confident man from the South Side of Chicago who took great pride in his work.

Months went by, and the case began to stall. However on a quiet Saturday morning, I received a call that a man had been arrested after a noise complaint at a local hotel. Police searched his room and found counterfeit bills with serial numbers matching those from my case. The name of the man in custody? Arthur Williams Jr.

I headed straight to the police station to interview the man I knew as Art. Honestly, I didn't have much to go on. I knew where the fake bills had been passed and on what dates, but little else. I wasn't experienced, and I didn't look like a seasoned agent. Still, I knew I had to project confidence.

More importantly, I knew I couldn't fake experience. So, I relied on something else: curiosity. What others had told me about Art stuck with me—he had a strong sense of pride in his skills and a deep need for respect. I decided to tap into that. I reminded myself of Dale Carnegie's timeless advice: "Be interested to be interesting." My goal wasn't to confront Art—it was to connect.

When we met, I told him I had flown in from Washington, D.C., on the agency's Gulfstream jet. I hoped this would boost my credibility in his eyes. In reality, I had driven my beat-up government-issued 1991 Plymouth Acclaim. I wanted him to believe he was worth the time. A peasant couldn't catch Robin Hood—he needed to be caught by the sheriff. I praised the quality of his work, telling him it was the some of the best counterfeit we'd ever seen. His posture shifted. A smirk crossed his face. I knew I had his attention.

We started by talking about his upbringing on the South Side. Then I leaned into the principle of curiosity. I asked about his counterfeiting process—what kind of paper he used, what kind of glue held it together, and how he sourced his supplies, etc. His eyes lit up. For the next hour, he became a professor, teaching me his process, step by step. Every mistake, every discovery, every trick.

Eventually, he admitted to printing several hundred thousand dollars' worth of counterfeit bills. He also mentioned that he was writing a book about his life and working on a movie script. I told him I couldn't wait to read it and even asked who should portray him in the film. This curiosity sprinkled with validation was the recipe that was needed.

Art was later charged with manufacturing and possessing counterfeit currency and faced serious prison time. However, there was an issue with how the local police searched his hotel room, leading to the case being dismissed immediately and Art being a free man.

Art moved to Alaska to reconnect with his father, but the pull of his old lifestyle was strong. Unable to resist, he returned to counterfeiting—this time with his father's help. When his father was arrested by Secret Service agents in Alaska, he turned on Art to protect himself. This time, there was no technicality to help him, and he served several years in federal prison.

After his release, Art returned to Chicago. I didn't expect to ever see him again—until a co-worker called and told me to check out the latest issue of *Rolling Stone*. There, inside the magazine, was a full-page depiction of Art's face, printed on a $100 bill. The article hailed him as the "King of Counterfeit" and claimed he had gone straight.

That same week, our office received a large batch of counterfeit bills from local merchants and banks. As soon as I examined them, I knew they belonged to him. The technique, the ink, the subtle details—all bore Art's signature style. We reopened the case. Then a couple of months later, while under surveillance, Art's teenage son had an outburst. After a heated argument, he ran into the street and threw a handful of counterfeit bills onto the windshield of a Chicago Police car. It led to their arrest and a search of their home. Inside, we discovered a fully operational counterfeit lab.

I interviewed Art's son, who openly admitted to helping with the operation. In less than five years, Art had now been betrayed by both his father and his son.

Armed with information provided by his son, I came up with a familiar strategy for my interview with Art. I knew I had to play to his sense of pride once again. I told him I had flown in on a newer, more advanced Secret Service jet. I complimented him on the improved quality of his latest work and asked for his autograph on the depiction of his face on the $100 bill in the *Rolling Stone* article. He grinned, signed it, and wrote, *"To Brad, the greatest Secret Service agent ever – Arthur Williams Jr."*

We sat down again. I asked him how he had subtly changed his counterfeit process this time, including how he used an offset printer and sourced a color-shifting ink similar to that on real currency. Once again, curiosity opened the door—no pressure, no fear, just respect and genuine interest.

He ultimately admitted to producing over $8 million in counterfeit currency. Months later, he was sentenced to nine years in federal prison. Years afterward, his son was arrested again for counterfeiting and ended up sharing a cell with his father. Upon release, Art achieved what many counterfeiters could not—staying clean and avoiding a return to counterfeiting. Instead, he began painting while in prison and upon his release became a popular artist.

What I learned from Art is that when people feel seen, valued, and respected—especially for their resilience, intelligence, or creativity—they are much more likely to open up. Whether you're conducting an interview, leading a team, mentoring, parenting, or just trying to connect with someone, the same principle holds. Ask with genuine interest and curiosity, and you'll see many doors open.

Curiosity may unlock the door, but the next step, *observation*, is what guides you through it with intention. The moment someone begins to open up, your attention must sharpen. What you observe in that moment—facial expressions, shifts in posture, hesitation in their voice—can reveal more than their words ever will.

O—OBSERVATION AS A COGNITIVE SUPERPOWER

Observation is more than simply seeing—it is an active cognitive process that allows individuals to decode subtle behavioral patterns, anticipate reactions, and shape outcomes. It is the skill that separates great communicators, negotiators, and law enforcement officers from the rest.

One of the most compelling studies proving the power of observation comes from Dr. Paul Ekman and Maureen O'Sullivan's Wizards Project research study. This study tested 20,000 professionals—including law enforcement officers, psychologists, and attorneys—on their ability to detect deception. The results? Most people scored just 54% accuracy—barely better than random chance. However, one group stood out: Secret Service Agents.

Unlike interrogators trained to catch lies, Secret Service Agents are trained to detect threats in real time. Their ability to read body language, scan for anomalies, and identify behavioral incongruities allowed them to outperform every other group. Of the 20,000 participants, only 50 achieved an 80% accuracy rate—a group Ekman labeled "Truth Wizards"[5]

The ability to read subtle shifts in body language, tone, and facial expressions allows skilled communicators to anticipate objections, detect hidden emotions, and adjust their approach accordingly in real time. While some individuals—like Secret Service Agents and elite negotiators—develop superior observational skills through experience, anyone can train themselves to become a better observer.

Here are proven methods, backed by psychology, neuroscience, and behavioral analysis, that will improve your ability to notice and interpret key social cues, which can be achieved through several evidence-based strategies. Below are specific steps, each supported by relevant statistics and studies.

Reduce Distractions—Put the Phone Away

The mere presence of a smartphone can significantly impair cognitive performance and interpersonal awareness. A 2015 study published in the *Journal of the Association for Consumer Research* found that participants with smartphones in sight experienced a 20% reduction in available cognitive capacity compared to those who kept their phones out of sight.[6]

When speaking to groups about communication, I frequently reference these studies to highlight the impact of smartphone presence on interaction quality. Simply placing your phone in another room can improve your engagement by 20%—without additional effort. Keeping your phone with you during a conversation is not only disrespectful but also disruptive, even if it is on silent. A vibrating phone in your hand, pocket, or on the table creates unnecessary distractions, breaking focus for both you and the speaker, ultimately hindering the flow and effectiveness of the conversation.

Maintain Eye Contact and Full-Body Observation

Effective observation goes beyond eye contact to encompass full-body language, essential for precise communication. In today's society, many people show poor eye contact, often due to increased reliance on digital communication and distractions of mobile devices. Research indicates that lack of eye contact can reduce perceived credibility and trustworthiness by up to 30%.[7] When you frequently look away or fail to make eye contact, it can signal disinterest, disrespect, or discomfort—while also blinding you to critical, real-time feedback.

That feedback often comes through body language, which serves as a gauge for how well your message is being received. I first became deeply aware of this when communicating with my best friend Doug, who is deaf. In our conversations, I have to be fully present—observing his reactions, avoiding assumptions, and adjusting my message if I sense confusion or disconnection. The same principle applies when I'm teaching or giving a presentation. I scan the room for subtle cues; a puzzled expression or furrowed brow indicates I need to clarify. Conversely, body language that opens up or a small nod of understanding reassures me that I'm connecting.

Unfortunately, too many people miss these cues—whether it's a presenter reading directly from their PowerPoint slides without ever looking at the audience or someone holding a personal conversation while gazing off into the distance. This behavior robs us of the silent, immediate feedback that makes real-time communication so effective. Observing the person or group you're speaking with allows you to tailor your message on the fly, increasing clarity and connection.

That doesn't mean you need to maintain constant, unbroken eye contact—which can come across as aggressive or unnatural. Instead, keep the other person's entire frame within your field of vision. This enables you to notice the subtle shifts: a change in posture, a clenched jaw, fidgeting hands—all signals of agreement, tension, or uncertainty. Adopting this full-spectrum awareness sharpens both your verbal and nonverbal communication, creating more meaningful, precise, and effective interactions.

Use a Second Observer in High-Stakes Conversations

The human brain is not equipped to handle multiple complex tasks at the same time, and trying to do so often leads to errors, especially in high-pressure or emotionally intense situations. Studies in cognitive load theory indicate that when people split their attention among various tasks, it can be detrimental to the accuracy of their decision-making abilities.[8] This is especially relevant in critical conversations, such as interviews, negotiations, or interrogations, where missing subtle nonverbal cues can alter the course of the interaction.

One strategy to mitigate this limitation is to incorporate a second observer into the conversation if appropriate. When gaining insight into the other person's emotions, intentions, or deception is crucial, one person should lead the discussion while another strictly observes. This approach can dramatically improve the ability to detect inconsistencies, emotional shifts, or stress reactions. The lead communicator can focus entirely on engagement and verbal exchange. At the same time, the observer dedicates their attention to monitoring nonverbal cues, such as changes in posture and variations in vocal tone.

This approach is widely used in law enforcement, where one investigator takes the primary role of questioning while another silently observes, noting behavioral shifts that may indicate deception, discomfort, or truthfulness.[9] In negotiations, having a secondary team member observe can provide crucial feedback on the opposing party's level of confidence or hesitation, informing strategic adjustments. By delegating responsibilities in this way, both individuals enhance the overall effectiveness of the conversation, reducing cognitive overload and increasing the likelihood of an accurate and insightful interpretation of the interaction.

Case Study: Observation in Action—From Trash Can to Confession

One particular case significantly changed my perspective on investigative work and deepened my appreciation for the power of observation and the art of interviewing.

During the 2000 presidential election, I was assigned to conduct protective intelligence advance for a campaign stop by then–Republican candidate George W. Bush in a medium-sized town in Illinois. My responsibilities included arriving several days before the visit to coordinate with local law enforcement and develop a plan to mitigate threats to the protective site. The week leading up to the visit was uneventful. However, the day before the visit, the local Republican headquarters received a voicemail from an unknown male caller threatening then-Governor Bush—a direct threat that demanded immediate attention and had the potential to significantly alter our resource allocation and protective strategy.

Fortunately, I was joined by Bill, a 20-year veteran Secret Service Agent whose investigative instincts would soon prove invaluable.

Our first objective was to determine the origin of the call. After consulting with the phone company, we traced it to a pay phone at a local strip mall. When we arrived at the location, we learned there was no surveillance footage available. I assumed this was a dead end. But Bill, drawing on his years of field experience, wasn't so quick to dismiss the scene. Instead, he began scanning the surrounding area—and made his first key observation: a nearby overflowing trash can positioned close to where employees often took their smoke breaks. While most would have ignored it, Bill walked over and began carefully sifting through the contents—dirty diapers, food wrappers, banana peels.

I watched in disbelief, thinking it was pointless. But then he paused, pulling out a small Styrofoam coffee cup. Inside, he found a folded piece of yellow notebook paper—the second observation. Written on it was a phone number. We unfolded it: It was the number for the Republican headquarters, directly linking the cup to the threatening call.

With less than 12 hours before Governor Bush's scheduled arrival, Bill sprang into action. We canvassed every gas station within a mile of the pay phone, checking to see if any carried cups that matched the one found in the trash. No luck. Then we visited a grocery store located near the pay phone. Knowing the time the call had been made, Bill hoped surveillance footage might reveal someone entering or exiting around that time.

While he spoke with the store manager in the employee break room about reviewing the tapes, Bill made another key visual observation: a stack of Styrofoam coffee cups in the break area—identical to the one found in the trash. Right beside it sat a yellow notepad with a missing page—its tear marks perfectly matching the one recovered earlier. Bill took it all in silently, processing every visual cue.

Then came the next key clue: a phone book left open on a side table, with the number for the Republican headquarters underlined in pen—yet another indicator we were in the right place.

Bill asked which male employees had been working during that shift and narrowed the list to three possible suspects. He then reviewed their employment applications, this time using a detail that would elude most people: He compared the handwriting on the applications to the note we found, looking for distinctive features. The first application he reviewed matched exactly—unique loops in the 2s and a curved style to the 7s made the match unmistakable.

The manager confirmed the man, let's call him "John," had worked at the store for years, was politically outspoken, and often made impulsive remarks when frustrated—but had never shown signs of violence.

We immediately responded to the suspect's home, accompanied by local law enforcement. With time running out and little room for error, we didn't have the luxury of a full background check. I remember watching Bill walk confidently to the front door of the suspect's house around 9 PM. His wife answered, and after we identified ourselves, she allowed us inside.

Then came Bill's final—and perhaps most human—observation. As we entered the modest home, he scanned the surroundings for emotional context. On the wall in the living room was a wedding photo—clearly aged—showing the suspect and his wife on their wedding day. Next to it was a framed picture of the suspect in military uniform, unmistakably from the Vietnam era. Bill understood the power of empathy and connection—and he stored that detail for the moment it would matter most.

He sat down across from the suspect, calm and composed, and began:

"John, the Secret Service does two things: We investigate individuals who counterfeit money, and we protect the president of the United States. Have you counterfeited any money recently?"

The suspect replied, "No."

"Well, now you know why we're here," Bill said. Then, drawing from what he had seen moments earlier, he softened his tone and continued, "By all accounts, you're a good family man who's obviously been married for many years—and someone who has served this country. I don't think you're the kind of man who would intentionally hurt anyone."

The suspect lowered his head and began to cry. He confessed to making the call following a heated political discussion at work.

We arrested him, confiscated his firearms, and the protective visit of Governor Bush proceeded without incident.

Witnessing this master class in investigative interviewing—fueled not by hunches or aggression but by quiet, deliberate observation and emotional intelligence—inspired me to develop similar skills. That moment was one of the defining reasons I pursued certification as a polygraph examiner with the Secret Service. I wanted to be as effective and insightful as Bill. Observation is a silent superpower. The next step? Using that information with *respect*.

R—RESPECT: THE TRUST MULTIPLIER

While establishing rapport is often emphasized in communication, it is equally important to respect the individual. Rapport can be elusive in certain situations due to personality clashes or situational factors. However, respect can sometimes transcend these differences. Much of it involves understanding Maslow's Hierarchy of Needs, which explains ensuring safety and meeting basic needs are foundational before achieving higher levels of interaction.[10]

Becoming friends with someone typically requires a significant investment of time and interaction. According to a study by Jeffrey Hall, it takes 40 to 60 hours of shared time to form a casual friendship, 80 to 100 hours to transition to a true friendship, and over 200 hours to become close friends.[11] These findings emphasize the importance of spending quality time together and participating in various activities to deepen the friendship bond.

Given the time required to establish true friendship, focusing on obtaining respect during interactions becomes crucial. When individuals feel their basic needs are met and their immediate safety is assured, they are more likely to respect the interviewer for meeting this requirement.

In my current profession, I train people to elicit information from people who have chosen to break the law. One of my core teaching principles is to treat the person across from me with the utmost respect. Respect is essential regardless of their background, political views, or actions. This approach aligns with the Platinum Rule coined by Dr. Tony Alessandra: Treat others how *they* prefer to be treated, not just how *you* would like to be treated.[12]

I recall a specific child exploitation case where we served a search warrant at a suspect's residence during winter. The suspect had to wait outside in shorts and bare feet while the search was conducted. When I approached him, I saw him shivering from the freezing temperatures. I returned to his house and brought him his boots, pants, and a large parka. He was visibly grateful for this gesture. Later, during an interview at the police station, he made significant criminal admissions, which ultimately led to a long prison sentence. After his confession, I asked him a question I routinely pose at the end of an interaction: "Why did you choose to tell me the truth?" He responded, "Because you treated me like a human being."

A friend of mine, Martin, is a retired FBI agent and a world-class interrogator. He maintains that every suspect—regardless of their demeanor or the severity of their alleged crime—deserves to be treated with such dignity that, ideally, they would feel compelled to send him a Christmas card from prison. And despite these people having gone to prison as a result of speaking with Martin, many did in fact send Christmas cards to his FBI field office over the years. Whether negotiating a business deal, testifying in court, or interviewing a suspect, people respond better when they feel valued as human beings. Respect doesn't mean agreement—it means acknowledgment.

This principle mirrors the techniques used during World War II by Hanns Scharff, a renowned Luftwaffe interrogator. Scharff developed a technique of interrogation based on respect, empathy, and nonconfrontation that is still used today. Instead of force or intimidation, Scharff's approach involved calm observation, active listening, and courteous engagement. His technique was highly effective in extracting crucial information and defied the harsh expectations that many airmen had of interrogations. Several individuals he interrogated later became his friends after he immigrated to the United States following the war.[13]

Years ago, I attended a speaking engagement with former FBI agent George Piro, who shared his experience interrogating Saddam Hussein. Piro established a deep connection with Hussein, even getting him addicted to the cookies his mother shipped him from the United States. Hussein reportedly cried when Piro's time with him ended. He didn't cry because Piro forced a confession but because Piro fostered a relationship. Respect can be the difference between silence and confession, resistance and cooperation, even with your enemies. Building this connection requires time, genuine interest, and validation of the other person's interests.

These three individuals' methods emphasize the importance of dignity and respect even in the most challenging circumstances. They produced effective and morally sound results by treating subjects as human beings, not adversaries.

By offering value first, whether through time, information, or goodwill, we naturally encourage others to respond in kind. This mutual exchange transforms relationships from transactional to meaningful, reinforcing trust and fostering long-term influence. Now, let's explore how *exchange* in the form of reciprocity serves as a powerful commitment trigger in communication.

E—EXCHANGE (RECIPROCITY): THE COMMITMENT TRIGGER

In the realm of influence, one principle stands out for its simplicity and profound impact: reciprocity. This fundamental concept dictates that when someone provides us with something—whether it's a favor, information, or even a simple gesture—we feel a powerful, often subconscious, urge to return the favor. This inherent human tendency to reciprocate forms the bedrock of numerous social interactions and significantly influences our decisions.[14]

The Mechanism Behind the Obligation

Once this internal "debt mechanism" is activated, we instinctively feel obligated to balance the scales when we receive something, creating a sense of indebtedness that compels us to reciprocate. This feeling is not necessarily a conscious calculation but rather a deeply ingrained social norm that drives our behavior. Dr. Robert Cialdini famously demonstrated that people are significantly more likely to comply with requests after receiving something from the requester first.[15]

To leverage reciprocity effectively, the key is to be willing to give first without expecting immediate returns. This can manifest in various forms, from offering a kind word or gesture of appreciation to providing tangible goods or services. By initiating the exchange with generosity, we cultivate an environment of trust and goodwill that naturally encourages others to reciprocate.

Reciprocity in Action: Personal Anecdotes

The simplicity of reciprocity makes it a potent tool in various contexts. Throughout my career, I've witnessed its effectiveness time and again.

- **Diplomatic Encounters:** I was paired with a Japanese counterpart from their dignitary protection team during a presidential trip to Japan. Over four days, we developed a genuine rapport. On the final day, I presented him with a souvenir Secret Service lapel pin as a token of appreciation. In response, he offered me his father's antique cuff links, a gift of immense personal value. Despite my attempts to decline, he insisted, explaining that refusing would be a profound act of disrespect. This exchange underscored the powerful sense of obligation that reciprocity can create. Reciprocity isn't just psychological; it's cross-cultural. The key is to give first without expecting immediate returns. Over time, those small gestures build lasting influence.

- **International Security:** Similarly, while assigned to the protection detail of Iranian president Mahmoud Ahmadinejad during his first visit to the United Nations, I gifted their detail leader a souvenir lapel pin before their departure. In return, he presented me with his official Iranian protection lapel pin. These instances demonstrate that reciprocity transcends cultural boundaries and applies even in high-stakes diplomatic and security settings.
- **Everyday Interactions:** Beyond material gifts, reciprocity governs our daily interactions. Offering food, drink, and basic courtesies to everyone I interact with, regardless of their alleged crimes, demonstrates this principle. Sharing information, time, and generosity cultivates a positive feedback loop, fostering mutual respect and cooperation.

Of all the principles of influence, reciprocity benefits immensely from its inherent simplicity. Its effectiveness stems from the fundamental human desire to maintain balance and fairness in our interactions. By understanding and applying this principle, we can build stronger relationships, foster cooperation, and enhance our ability to influence others ethically and effectively.

Social proof builds confidence in decisions, curiosity fosters understanding and engagement, observation uncovers unspoken cues, respect strengthens trust and cooperation, and exchange reinforces reciprocity. When consistently applied, these elements make persuasion a natural outcome of authentic relationships, ensuring your influence is powerful and enduring.

In my interactions with thousands of criminals, I would get close to people, learn from them, and then *sometimes* feel a brief moment of sadness when they were arrested after disclosing their crimes to me. Spending time with people discussing sensitive matters creates a connection, even with those who have committed heinous acts. This underscores the profound impact of these SCORE principles because it can work for and against us. The more time I spend with these people conversing about their interests, the more they go from being a suspect to being a person.

A key takeaway is the power of this principle and how people will maliciously utilize these principles in personal and professional relationships to their benefit.

At the end of the day, persuasion isn't about manipulation—it's about ethically guiding people toward mutual benefit. Apply these principles in your next negotiation, leadership talk, or everyday conversation. Notice how trust and genuine rapport transform the outcome.

Yet, influence isn't just about what you say—it's about how well you listen. The most effective communicators don't dominate conversations; they create space for others to be heard. This is where active listening becomes essential. By truly hearing and understanding others, you not only gain valuable insight but also foster deeper connections.

CHAPTER 11

Active Listening and Mimicry

"Most people do not listen with the intent to understand; they listen with the intent to reply."
—Stephen Covey

In Stephen Covey's widely popular *The 7 Habits of Highly Successful People*, listening, especially active listening, is one of those habits.[1] However, it is one of the most underutilized soft skills. There is so much evidence to demonstrate its effectiveness, but we are often so caught up in our own thoughts that we aren't good listeners. Listening requires fully concentrating, understanding, responding, and remembering what is said.

One of the easiest ways to improve your ability to listen—and influence—is by using a framework I call SEEMS. It's a simple, repeatable approach that helps you stay present, build rapport, and guide conversations to meaningful outcomes. It's an acronym for Summarizing, Empathetic statements, Emotion labeling, Minimal encouragers, and Signal of interest. Here's how it works.

S—SUMMARIZING

Listening is not just about hearing words—it's about ensuring the other person knows they have been heard. That's where summarizing comes into play. It demonstrates that you were listening and can help clarify the speaker's thoughts.

I often use this principle to calm people down, and in many situations, I find that their primary concern is not what I expected. Summarizing confirms we are both on the same page, and if I make incorrect assumptions, I provide them with a chance to clarify.

When you summarize, you show the speaker that you are actively engaged in the conversation. This demonstrates that you value their input and are committed to understanding their perspective. It also encourages the speaker to continue sharing more information.[2]

Summarizing Examples

- "It sounds like you're feeling . . ."
- "So, what you're saying is . . ."
- "So, your primary concern is . . ."

E—EMPATHETIC STATEMENTS

Understanding someone's words is one thing—grasping their emotions is quite another. This is where empathy becomes crucial. By acknowledging a person's feelings, you construct a bridge of trust and foster an environment where they feel secure enough to share more. Doing so can:

- **Build Trust and Rapport:** Demonstrating empathy fosters trust and rapport between you and the speaker. It cultivates a safe and supportive environment where the speaker feels valued and understood. Moreover, it validates the speaker's emotions, which is essential as it shows you acknowledge and respect their feelings, providing immense comfort and reassurance.

- **Promote Open Communication:** When speakers feel their emotions are being understood and respected, they are more likely to open up and share information. It can also help reduce the speaker's emotional distress. When someone feels heard and understood, their anxiety and stress levels often decrease, making them feel more at ease.[3]

Empathetic Statement Examples

- "I can see that this is important to you."
- "I can understand why you would feel that way."
- "That must have been really tough on you."
- "I see why this is so important to you."
- "It sounds like you had a crazy day."

E—EMOTION LABELING

Emotion labeling involves identifying and naming the emotions the speaker expresses, which helps to validate their feelings. By naming these emotions, you acknowledge their experience, making them feel understood and respected. This validation makes the speaker feel heard and valued. When you accurately identify and label someone's emotions, it builds trust and rapport, making the speaker feel that you genuinely want to understand their perspective. Naming emotions can help reduce their emotional distress intensity. Research suggests that putting feelings into words can diminish their power and make them more manageable. This process, known as affect labeling, can help individuals feel more in control of their emotions.[4]

Emotion Labeling Examples

- "You seem really excited about that opportunity."
- "It sounds like you're feeling a little overwhelmed."
- "I can sense that you're anxious about the new boss."

M—MINIMAL ENCOURAGERS

Minimal encouragers are small verbal and nonverbal cues that show engagement and encourage the speaker to continue talking. These cues significantly enhance communication and interpersonal relationships.[5] Minimal encouragers are increasingly vital in today's communication landscape. With a reliance on non-dynamic mediums such as text and email, people have grown accustomed to processing conversations at their own pace before responding. However, this skill set is often lacking when engaging in real-time conversations, which significantly impacts effective communication.

Utilizing minimal encouragers proves crucial when transitioning to face-to-face or live conversations. These subtle cues, such as nods and brief verbal acknowledgments, play a key role in fostering engagement and understanding in interpersonal interaction

There are two main reasons minimal encouragers are essential.

- **They Demonstrate Active Listening:** Using these cues shows you are paying attention to and value the speaker's words. This creates a supportive and empathetic environment. Speakers who feel listened to and understood are likelier to express themselves openly and honestly.

- **They Reduce Speaker Anxiety:** Speakers often feel anxious or uncertain, especially in sensitive or high-stakes conversations. Minimal encouragers can reassure them that their message is being received positively, reducing anxiety and fostering more confident communication.

Minimal Encourager Examples

- "I see."

- "Right."

- "Interesting."

- "That makes sense."
- "Go on . . ."
- "Uh-huh."
- "Sure."
- "Okay."

S—SIGNALS OF INTEREST

Signals of interest are verbal and nonverbal cues demonstrating that you are fully engaged in the conversation, fostering openness and encouraging continued communication. There are several reasons signals of interest are essential.

- **Build Trust and Rapport:** Showing genuine interest helps build trust and rapport between participants, creating a positive and supportive environment where both parties feel valued and respected.
- **Encourage Continued Sharing:** These signals encourage the speaker to continue sharing their thoughts and feelings. They act as prompts that keep the conversation flowing smoothly and prevent awkward pauses.
- **Boost Speaker Confidence:** When a speaker feels that their message is being received with interest, it boosts their confidence. This is particularly important in sensitive or highly emotional conversations.

Verbal Examples

- "Tell me more about that."
- "What happened next?"
- "What do you think about . . . ?"
- "How did you handle that situation?"

Nonverbal Examples

- Nodding.
- Leaning forward.
- Maintaining eye contact.
- Facial expressions that reflect understanding (smiling, concerned look).
- Fronting alignment (facing the speaker directly).
- Putting your phone down.
- Lack of judgment (maintaining an open and accepting demeanor).

THE ROLE OF MIMICRY IN ENHANCING COMMUNICATION

Too often, those who study body language approach it primarily as a tool for spotting deception—a use that has little scientific basis. In my experience, its greatest value lies elsewhere: in gauging another person's level of comfort or discomfort. Body language provides a real-time window into emotional states, often revealing what words cannot. When I sense someone is uncomfortable—through crossed arms, averted gaze, or closed posture—I don't just observe; I act. I deliberately use my own body language as a subtle guide, mirroring open and relaxed postures to encourage the other person to unconsciously adopt a more receptive stance. This gentle, nonverbal prompting fosters trust and authentic communication.

Listening is not just about hearing words; it is about creating a sense of being understood. Mimicry—a subtle yet powerful behavioral phenomenon—serves as a key conduit for this feeling. When we mirror another person's gestures, tone, or phrasing, we send an unspoken message: "I see you. I hear you. We are in sync." This phenomenon, known as the chameleon effect, is deeply embedded in our neurobiological makeup.[6]

Dr. Abbie Maroño, a close friend and leading expert in nonverbal behavior, has conducted groundbreaking research demonstrating the power of mimicry. Her findings indicate that the closer we feel emotionally to someone, the more likely we are to imitate them—and the more we are imitated, the closer we tend to feel. This creates a reinforcing cycle of connection and cooperation.

Her research also highlights which types of mimicry are most effective in building interpersonal connections. Whole-body mimicry, rather than just upper-body gestures, has a significantly stronger impact on feelings of closeness and cooperation. In particular, subtle lower-body mirroring has proven especially effective in fostering trust. This includes actions such as crossing the legs or ankles, aligning one's posture, or matching the direction of the other person's feet. In contrast, arm mimicry tends to be the least effective, likely because it is more visible and often serves a separate expressive function—making it easier to detect and less likely to be perceived as a genuine mimicry cue.[7]

When strategically employed in conversations, mimicry significantly strengthens rapport, cultivates openness, and amplifies influence—making it a critical extension of the active listening principles outlined earlier.

Subtle vs. Obvious Mimicry: The Nuance of Connection

The efficacy of mimicry hinges on its subtlety. While subtle mirroring fosters trust and rapport, overt or forced mimicry often elicits feelings of discomfort and manipulation. The key lies in seamlessly integrating your behavior with the other person's in a natural manner.

Subtle Mimicry Techniques

- **Posture and Gestures:** If the other person leans forward, subtly mirror this posture. If they employ hand gestures, incorporate similar gestures into your own repertoire, ensuring a delayed and natural execution.
- **Speech Patterns:** Adjust your tone, pace, and volume to align with theirs. Individuals who speak rapidly often feel more comfortable in high-energy conversations, while those who speak slowly appreciate a more measured approach.

- **Facial Expressions:** If they smile, reciprocate with a subtle smile. If they appear concerned, convey appropriate empathy through your facial expressions.

Pitfalls to Avoid

Even when engaging in subtle mimicry, there are several key pitfalls to avoid.

- **Immediate Mirroring:** Instantaneous copying of another person's actions often appears inauthentic, even mocking, hindering rapport.[8] In interview training, I frequently observe participants reflexively mirroring interviewees—crossing arms or legs the moment the other person does. This overt imitation disrupts natural interaction, signaling a lack of genuine connection. Instead of building trust, it can raise suspicion. Subtlety and timing are paramount; effective mimicry should be a delayed, nuanced reflection, not a direct replication.
- **Exaggerated Mimicry:** Exaggerated mimicry undermines sincerity and can easily be perceived as mockery. In practical exercises, I consistently observe trainees mimicking dramatic movements—large, obvious shifts in posture or gestures—from their subjects. These overt imitations are readily recognized, breaking the subtle illusion of connection. Instead of mirroring every large gesture, I advocate for more nuanced alignment. For instance, instead of directly mirroring crossed legs or arms, consider subtle variations like crossing your feet or hands. This approach maintains a sense of mirroring while avoiding the appearance of blatant imitation, preserving authenticity and fostering genuine rapport.
- **Mirroring Extreme Agitation:** It's essential to recognize that mirroring someone in a highly agitated state can be counterproductive. If a person exhibits intense anger, fear, or distress, directly reflecting these emotions can escalate the situation. Instead,

use mimicry to help guide them toward a calmer state. Start by acknowledging their feelings, then gradually adjust your demeanor to a more relaxed and reassuring one.[9]

Mimicry as a Tool for Guiding Conversations

Mimicry extends beyond simply building rapport; it serves as a powerful tool for subtly guiding conversations toward desired outcomes. This strategic use of mimicry leverages individuals' subconscious tendency to mirror those they perceive as similar or connected to. Here are some tips for how to do it well.

Initial Mirroring

Begin by subtly adopting aspects of the other person's posture, tone, or phrasing to establish a connection. This initial mirroring creates a sense of familiarity and trust, making the other person more receptive to your influence. This aligns with the "chameleon effect," where individuals unconsciously mimic others' postures, facial expressions, and mannerisms. This is supported by research showing that people tend to like those who are similar to themselves.[10]

Gradual Shifting

Once rapport is established, subtly adjust your own tone, posture, and demeanor to guide the other person toward a calmer, more receptive state. For example, if they are initially agitated, gradually shift to a more relaxed posture, a slower rate of speaking, and a calmer tone of voice. This technique is built on the concept that once a connection is established, the other person's limbic system will tend to synchronize with yours.[11] This also works because of the concept of emotional contagion, where emotional states are transferred between individuals.[12]

Facilitating Following

At its core, mimicry strengthens the active listening techniques previously discussed. When executed with finesse, mimicry serves as a silent yet powerful amplifier of trust and influence, seamlessly integrating with the fundamental principles of active listening to forge profound and meaningful connections.

Thanks to the subconscious influence of mimicry, they will often mirror your shifts without conscious awareness. This allows you to subtly guide the conversation toward a desired outcome, such as a more collaborative or solution-oriented mindset. This is observed in negotiation scenarios, where mirroring can lead to greater cooperation and agreement.[13] This is also seen in therapeutic settings, where mimicking a client's emotional state, then calmly shifting, can help de-escalate anxiety.

Consider a high-stakes negotiation or meeting where the other person enters the room feeling agitated and defensive. Directly mirroring their aggression will likely worsen the conflict. Instead, start with subtle alignment in tone, pace, and posture. Gradually slow your speech, lower your volume, and adopt a more relaxed posture. Thanks to the subconscious influence of mimicry, they will often begin to mirror these calming cues—without even realizing it. Over time, their breathing slows, their tone softens, and their body language opens up. What started as a tense standoff can shift into a productive dialogue, simply because you took the lead in regulating the emotional rhythm of the room.

PUTTING IT ALL TOGETHER

Let's imagine a scenario where a coworker is discussing a challenging project.

Coworker: (Leans forward, hands gesturing emphatically): "I've been really on edge about this new project. With the deadline approaching, I feel like there's so much to do and not enough time."

You: (Summarizing, leaning slightly forward, matching their tone): "It sounds like you're feeling stressed by the amount of work and a tight deadline."

Coworker: (Nods, voice slightly raised): "Exactly, and I'm not sure how to prioritize everything. It's just so much to get done."

You: (Empathy, maintaining eye contact, speaking in a slightly softer tone): "I can understand why it would be stressful for you. It's tough to handle so many tasks at once. Especially with everything else you have going on."

Coworker: (Crosses arms, voice tense): "Yes, and I'm worried that I won't be able to meet my manager's crazy expectations."

You: (Mimic, slightly mirroring their arm position, using a similar tone): "Crazy demands?"

Coworker: (Voice rising): "Yeah, he wants us to work on this 14 hours a day!"

You: (Empathy, widening your eyes slightly, feigning disbelief): "Fourteen hours a day, no way?"

Coworker: (Sighs, uncrossing arms): "Yeah. It's insane."

You: (Emotion labeling, voice calming, posture relaxing slightly): "It sounds like you're feeling anxious about completing everything on time."

Coworker: (Nods, voice softening): "That's right. I don't want to let the team down."

You: (Minimal encouragers, using a gentle nod and matching their quieter tone): "I see. That makes sense. What part of the project is causing you the most stress?"

Coworker: "It's the data analysis. It's so time-consuming, and I'm worried I'll miss some little detail."

You: (Summarizing and offering support): "So, the data analysis is the biggest hurdle, and you're concerned about accuracy. Would it help if we brainstormed some ways to streamline that process or if I took a look at the data with you?"

Coworker: (Eyes brightening slightly): "That would be awesome! I didn't want to bother you, but having another set of eyes would truly put my mind at ease."

You: (Empathetic tone): "You're not bothering me at all. We're a team, and we're here to support each other. I've dealt with similar situations before, so maybe I can offer some insights. How about we grab some coffee and go over it later today?"

Coworker: (Relief evident in their voice): "That sounds perfect. Thank you so much! I feel so much better."

You: (Positive reinforcement and closing): "You're welcome. We will get this sorted out in no time." (You offer a warm, genuine smile, maintaining eye contact.)

By using these techniques, you demonstrate active listening and give your coworker a sense of being heard and understood, which can help them feel more supported and less anxious about their situation. By combining the conscious techniques of active listening with the subconscious power of mimicry, particularly nonverbal mimicry, we can build trust and communicate much more effectively.

While we've explored how these tools can create trust and open communication, they also equip us to recognize when something feels amiss. The ability to notice subtle shifts in behavior and deviations from established patterns becomes crucial when navigating situations where honesty may be in question. Just as we learn to recognize signals of genuine connection, we can also learn to identify signals that may indicate deception.

PART IV

Detecting Deception and Uncovering Truth

How to Spot Lies, and Elicit the Truth

CHAPTER 12

Detecting Deception

"No mortal can keep a secret. If his lips are silent, he chatters with his fingertips; betrayal oozes out of him at every pore."
—Sigmund Freud

We live in a world where deception is everywhere—criminal interrogations, corporate negotiations, even everyday interactions. Despite our confidence in spotting liars, studies consistently show that the average person and even trained professionals are poor at detecting deception.

During my eight years at the National Center for Credibility Assessment, I had access to the world's most extensive research on deception detection. Yet, what I learned wasn't that there's a foolproof method to catch a liar—it's that deception is complex, fluid, and can mislead even the most experienced professionals.

The individuals most capable of detecting deception utilize a wide range of methods to achieve their goals. Throughout my years of research,

I've often encountered literature and courses where authors or presenters claim their approach is the industry standard. However, on what basis do they make these claims? Does research support them? I've come across authors who assert they can detect deception 99% of the time, secure a confession in every case, or close every sale. Such claims are mere snake oil sales pitches. Perfect systems and magical solutions do not exist.

However, I can confidently say that applying the principles discussed in this chapter can significantly enhance your ability to detect deception. Consider this analogy: The median batting average in Major League Baseball is .250, while an All-Star player typically has a .290 average. This means an average player succeeds 25 times out of 100, whereas an elite player succeeds 29 times out of 100. The difference between being average and being exceptional can often be relatively small. The key to detecting deception isn't fixating on lies—it's learning to recognize the truth. Most people know the Secret Service for protecting others, but the agency was originally established in 1865 to combat counterfeiting—a mission we still focus on today. In training, we don't start by studying fake money. We begin with the real thing. By learning every detail of genuine US currency—the paper, ink, layout, and texture—we develop the instincts to identify anything that's off. That lesson stayed with me: Counterfeits come in many forms, but genuine currency only exists in one form. The same idea applies to communication. Lies can take many shapes, but the truth usually follows a recognizable pattern. Once you become familiar with how truth sounds and feels in a conversation, it becomes easier to spot deviations.

The following sections will introduce practical techniques for improving deception detection and elicitation—small, incremental improvements that can significantly impact your effectiveness in negotiations, interviews, and everyday conversations.

In the realm of interviewing, I find it effective to draw an analogy that resonates with anyone who has ever had a dog. In the initial phase of the interaction, we employ a strategy akin to allowing a dog off its leash. By posing numerous open-ended questions, we allow the person we are speaking with to provide a spontaneous narrative, like a dog freely exploring its surroundings. While this approach encourages a comprehensive account, it comes with a caveat. There is a risk of the other party leading us astray, emphasizing truthful aspects while skillfully avoiding or omitting areas where they may not be forthcoming.

When we shift to using closed-ended questions, it is comparable to putting the dog back on a leash. We intentionally limit their range of movement, curtailing the potential for deviation from the intended path. By posing specific questions, we guide the interviewee's responses and, in doing so, create a scenario that could facilitate the detection of deception. However, it is essential to acknowledge the inherent limitation: The interviewee may not have the opportunity to clarify or elaborate on their responses to closed-ended questions.

Each approach has its strengths and weaknesses, and selecting the most appropriate method depends on the specific nuances of the interview and the information sought.

Humans lie frequently but don't want to be caught lying. Just as shifting between open-ended and closed-ended questions can reveal inconsistencies, physiological responses provide another layer of insight. This is where polygraphs come in. During a polygraph examination, I monitor a person's physiological responses, including electrodermal activity, respiration, and cardiac rate and quality, particularly in the 5–10 seconds following specific questions. These internal responses, indicative of deception, are invisible without a polygraph instrument. However, even without the instrument, it is essential to recognize that these physiological changes persist when someone is being deceptive.[1]

Deceptive individuals still exhibit increased electrodermal responses, alterations in breathing patterns, and changes in cardiac patterns and rate. These physiological changes and the additional cognitive load experienced during deception can lead to subtle cues that may reveal deceptive behavior. Knowing what to look for and understanding the specific time frame in which these changes occur enhances the ability to detect deception, even without the aid of a polygraph instrument.

MYTHS AND LACK OF ABSOLUTES WITH DETECTION OF DECEPTION

It is crucial to debunk certain myths associated with deception detection. Firstly, no singular "Pinocchio" trait is universally indicative of lying. It would be great if someone's nose would grow or if their pants caught on fire when they chose to be deceptive. However, numerous claims in countless books by purported experts tout specific cues as foolproof indicators—such assertions are fundamentally incorrect. The reality is that no one-size-fits-all characteristic serves as a definitive signal of deception.

Myths also surround micro-expressions. Some proponents suggest that detecting lies hinges on observing subtle facial expressions or unconscious linguistic patterns. However, the scientific validity of these claims remains questionable, and reliance on such cues as universal indicators of deception lacks empirical support.[2]

The myth that eye contact is a reliable indicator of deception is another misconception. Contrary to popular belief, the significance of eye contact varies among individuals and depends on the situation. The notion that someone is untrustworthy simply because they avoid eye contact oversimplifies the complex nature of human behavior. On the other hand, deceptive individuals may deliberately increase eye contact, exploiting the misconception that a heightened amount equates to honesty. The old saying "your lying eyes" is highly misleading.

For years, eye-accessing cues were taught throughout the law enforcement community. I still attend various conferences where speakers present this material. Eye-accessing cues are a concept that suggests individuals move their eyes in specific directions when recalling information versus fabricating it. However, recent studies have found no significant correlation between eye movement patterns and deception. Eye movement patterns can vary significantly among individuals and can be influenced by numerous factors, such as cognitive load, stress, and individual differences.[3]

Moreover, body language is an amazing field of study. Anyone who has read the work of former FBI agent Joe Navarro can understand the impact reading body language can have on furthering communication and detecting stress. However, Navarro points out that no research indicates body language correlates with deception. When someone crosses their arms or touches their nose while responding to a question, it may not be that they are deceptive. It is just as likely that they are cold, their nose itches, or you are making them uncomfortable.[4]

Conveying the truth is a straightforward process, akin to accessing a computer's memory bank and articulating the events as they occurred. When an individual is truthful, they effortlessly retrieve information from their mental "hard drive" and relay it. Picture it as a seamless recall, like a computer processing data.

However, the dynamics shift when someone is being deceptive. Knowing the truth, they must first suppress that reality. Subsequently, they construct a fabricated version, articulating the lie while simultaneously assessing your reaction to gauge its acceptance. This intricate mental process, termed cognitive load, involves:

- Suppressing the truth.
- Formulating a lie.
- Monitoring your response to see if their lie has been detected.

I teach my trainees to anticipate a prompt and unequivocal answer with specific questions that warrant a simple "yes" or "no" response. Any deviation from a straightforward "yes" or "no" raises a red flag. This approach highlights the principle that the cognitive load associated with deception frequently manifests in the response provided. The fear of getting caught leads to the psychological state of fight, flight, or freeze.

FIGHT, FLIGHT, AND FREEZE REACTION

When someone is caught in a lie, their body often reacts before their words do. The fight-or-flight response kicks in—heart rate increases, breathing shifts, pupils dilate, and muscles tense, as if preparing to confront a threat or escape it. Others may experience a "freeze" response, becoming unnaturally still in an unconscious attempt to avoid detection.

But here's the catch—stress and deception aren't the same. Just because someone appears nervous doesn't mean they're lying. A person under interrogation may exhibit clear fight-or-flight symptoms simply due to the high-stakes environment, not because they are guilty. This is why understanding baseline behavior is critical. Without it, we risk mistaking anxiety for deception.

No single behavior is definitive proof of dishonesty. Instead of relying on one isolated reaction, we must look for clusters of behaviors that emerge after specific questions. The challenge with using fight, flight, or freeze as a deception indicator is that stress alone can trigger these responses. Whether in a job interview, a high-pressure negotiation, or a criminal interrogation, significant life events naturally create anxiety. Distinguishing between stress and deception is key—otherwise, we risk misreading an honest person as a liar.

THE SPOTLIGHT EFFECT

The spotlight effect is the idea that people often believe others are paying more attention to them than they are. It's like imagining a spotlight shining on you, making you think everyone notices your actions, appearance, or mistakes. In truth, most people are focused on themselves and don't notice as much as we believe they do.[5]

When it comes to deception, the spotlight effect can play a significant role. When someone lies, they might feel like everyone can see right through their deception, as if a spotlight is exposing their every move. This feeling can increase their anxiety and stress, making them more likely to show signs of nervousness, like sweating or fidgeting. However, just like with the spotlight effect in other situations, the truth is that people usually aren't paying as much attention as the person thinks. Understanding the spotlight effect can help people manage their fears about being caught in a lie. However, it also shows why people might act suspiciously even if they aren't lying—they feel like they are under more scrutiny than they are.

In order to *increase* an individual's chances of correctly identifying when someone is lying, I developed the acronym DECEIVES. This helps an individual identify red flag behaviors that will aid in evaluating if further inquiry is needed. The key word is *assist*, as it is rare that one single statement or behavior will accurately indicate deception. However, when a person DECEIVES, they will likely engage in one or more of the following behaviors:

D—Delaying

E—Exclusive qualifiers

C—Confronting the questioner

E—Emotional inconsistency

I—Inserting truthful information into a lie

V—Verbal/nonverbal disconnect

E—Evading

S—Shifting vocal inflection

D—DELAYING

Based on my experience, one of the most common and telling indicators of verbal deception is answer latency—a noticeable delay between the question and the response. This delay often takes the form of the individual asking for the question to be repeated or pausing longer than their usual response pattern. While it may seem subtle, this hesitation often reflects cognitive load: The individual is mentally processing the question and how to answer it without incriminating themselves.

When someone tells the truth, the memory is readily accessible. But when lying, the person must construct a plausible answer, monitor the story for consistency, and manage their nonverbal cues—all of which increases cognitive burden and slows response time. This is especially true in high-stakes conversations where the cost of being caught in a lie is significant.[6]

Delays can also manifest as the subject repeating the question, even when it was clearly heard. In deceptive contexts, repeating the question may be a stall tactic, allowing extra time to fabricate or modify an answer. However, it's important to consider alternative explanations:

- Didn't understand the question.
- Is trying to provide a clear answer.
- Is genuinely trying to remember something that happened long ago.

As with all cues to deception, delays must be evaluated in context and compared against a subject's baseline behavior.

While conducting a routine polygraph examination for a law enforcement applicant who happened to work as a local firefighter, I experienced an unexpected turn of events. During the pre-polygraph interview, intriguing patterns emerged while obtaining a baseline for the applicant's verbal and nonverbal responses.

I was reviewing a checklist with the applicant, asking if he had ever participated in any activities related to criminal behavior. The subject exhibited a consistent response pattern with no noticeable delay as we progressed through the checklist. However, a clear deviation appeared when the inquiry turned to arson. In this instance, a significant delay, paired with a distinct lack of conviction in the subject's denial—expressed as a hesitant "noooo"—stood in stark contrast to the established baseline. The response nearly resembled a question rather than a straightforward denial.

At this point, my partner and I focused on this area of concern regarding arson. The applicant eventually admitted to intentionally setting fire to an abandoned building. His rationale was that he started the fire so that his unit could get real-world training. What began as a routine assessment for a law enforcement position transformed the applicant's trajectory significantly. The day commenced with aspirations of joining a prestigious agency and later concluded with the individual being arrested for arson.

This case serves as a powerful reminder that deceptive responses are often marked not just by what is said, but by how it is said. One common linguistic signal to watch for is the use of exclusive qualifiers.

E—EXCLUSIVE QUALIFYING

Exclusive qualifiers—words like "usually," "normally," "initially," "basically," and "probably"—are linguistic hedges that people often use to create psychological and semantic distance from their statements. These qualifiers allow the speaker to technically avoid a lie, while still misleading the listener. In the context of deception, this behavior is often subconscious and serves two main purposes:

1. To reduce cognitive dissonance.
2. To protect against potential accusation.

Lying creates internal psychological discomfort—a tension known as cognitive dissonance. This is the mental strain experienced when one's actions conflict with one's beliefs or identity.[7] Exclusive qualifiers help the liar manage this discomfort by adding wiggle room to their statements. It's a form of verbal distancing—not from the event, but from direct responsibility.

For example:

Q: "Did you visit that website?"

A: "I don't usually go to those kinds of sites."

The speaker hasn't said "no"—they've implied innocence without committing to a clear denial. This not only eases the internal stress of lying, but also gives them plausible deniability if confronted with contrary evidence later. Liars are more likely to use modifiers and qualifiers that soften the impact of their statements.[8]

When someone tells the truth, they tend to be direct and unqualified:

- "I didn't do it."
- "I've never been there."
- "That's not mine."

When someone is lying, they may unconsciously reach for language that grants them an escape hatch, such as:

- "I don't usually do that."
- "Normally, I follow this procedure."
- "Basically, I told him everything."
- "We probably left around ten."

This linguistic softening serves as an internal coping mechanism. It allows the liar to feel less as though they are delivering an outright falsehood and more as if they are simply shading the truth. In doing so, they alleviate the internal stress that typically accompanies deception. The more qualifiers and modifiers they insert, the more mental ground they preserve for themselves if their statement is later challenged. This creates a subtle escape hatch: they haven't technically lied, but they've shaped the message to serve their interests.

As previously discussed, lying is inherently uncomfortable and can trigger physiological stress responses—elevated heart rate, changes in vocal pitch, sweating, or body tension. By softening their language with exclusive qualifiers, liars buffer themselves against this internal discomfort. The more uncertain or elastic their language sounds, the more they attempt to manage both their outward impression and their own emotional state.

Recognizing these patterns of linguistic softening is critical, but they often appear alongside another deceptive behavior: shifting the pressure back onto the questioner. This brings us to the next red flag—confronting the questioner.

C—CONFRONTING THE QUESTIONER

Confronting the questioner is something people commonly do during sensitive conversations. It becomes a red flag for deception when someone is asked a fair question about their involvement in a situation and instead of answering with a straightforward "yes" or "no," they emotionally respond with something like:

- "It is ridiculous that you would accuse me of something like that."
- "How dare you ask me that question."
- "That's nuts!"
- "Who are you to accuse me of that?"
- "You must have no clue what you are doing."

If it is a fair question, you should get a fair response. When people feel like they're being backed into a corner because the truth is not on their side, they think they need to go on the attack and impeach the questioner's credibility.

Another similar defense mechanism is making the questioner into the villain. A fair question should not cause the questioner to be attacked. Lance Armstrong's denials about using performance enhancements and Richard Nixon's knowledge of the Watergate scandal both showcase this behavior.

Lance Armstrong's Response to Doping Allegations

- "We have nothing to hide. I think the real issue here is the credibility of the accuser." (Response to accusations, 2004)
- "The people who don't believe in cycling, the cynics, and the skeptics, I feel sorry for you. I'm sorry you can't dream big, and I'm sorry you don't believe in miracles." (2005 Tour de France victory speech)

Richard Nixon and the Watergate Scandal

- "The press is the enemy. The press is the enemy. The press is the enemy. Write that on a blackboard one hundred times and never forget it."
- "Don't get the impression that you arouse my anger. You see, one can only be angry with those he respects."

In both cases, Armstrong and Nixon avoided answering direct questions because the truth wasn't on their side. Instead of addressing the allegations head-on, they shifted tactics—choosing to attack their accusers or discredit the press as a means of deflection.

E—EMOTIONAL INCONSISTENCY

Lying requires constructing a false narrative, remembering fabricated details, and anticipating follow-up questions. This heightened cognitive demand can impair the liar's ability to control emotional expressions, leading to noticeable discrepancies between their words and emotions. Deceptive individuals must suppress truthful emotions and generate false ones, leading to emotional slips and inconsistencies, such as inappropriate laughter or a nervous smile, which betray their attempts to maintain a truthful facade.

A 2005 study analyzed videotaped statements from suspects in criminal cases to identify patterns of emotional inconsistency. The study found guilty individuals were significantly more likely to exhibit inappropriate nonverbal reactions, such as laughing or smiling when discussing serious charges, than innocent suspects. Many of these individuals displayed exaggerated emotions, such as sadness or remorse, which can appear performative rather than genuine. Investigators trained to recognize these emotional cues were more successful in distinguishing between truthful and deceptive suspects.[9]

Emotional inconsistency is frequently observed in individuals arrested for serious felony offenses. Often, while proclaiming their innocence, they laugh and smile—reactions that are highly inconsistent with the gravity of the situation. For example, imagine a SWAT team arriving at your house to conduct a search warrant at 6 AM. You are taken into custody and handcuffed. If you were innocent and your arrest was a mistake, laughing and smiling would be highly unusual responses.

Indicators of Fake Emotions

Several indicators can help differentiate between genuine and fake emotions.

- **Posture:** Genuine anger often involves a confrontational posture, with the person frontally aligned toward the source of anger. If someone is frontally aligned but showing signs of calmness, such as stomach breathing, it suggests a lack of genuine anger.
- **Breathing Patterns:** Calm, steady breathing is inconsistent with genuine anger, which usually causes shallow and rapid breathing due to the body's fight-or-flight response.[10]
- **Hand Gestures:** True anger is often accompanied by clenched fists or palms facing downward. If these gestures are absent, it can indicate that the displayed anger is not genuine.[11]

Research shows that genuine emotions usually unfold in a natural sequence—they build slowly, peak, and then gradually fade, mirroring the body's internal physiological state. It's similar to a dimmer switch being gently turned up or down, allowing emotions to brighten or dim in a smooth, consistent way.

Deceptive emotions, however, often lack this steady rhythm. They might appear out of nowhere, linger longer than feels natural, or disappear in an instant. These expressions can seem out of sync with the person's tone of voice or other nonverbal cues, creating a disconnect that raises suspicion.[12]

Case Study: R. Kelly

During an interview with Gayle King of *CBS This Morning*, R. Kelly was asked about the allegations of his having sexual relations with minors.

> **Gayle King:** "Have you ever had sex with anyone under the age of seventeen?"
>
> **R. Kelly:** "No. No. I sit here and say this. I had two cases back then that I said in the beginning of the interview that I would not talk about because of my ongoing case now. Fair enough. But I will tell you this: People are going back to my past—that's exactly what they're doing, they're going back to the past—and they're trying to add all of this stuff now to that, to make all of this stuff that's going on now feel real to people."

Kelly then escalated his response, standing up and becoming highly emotional, shouting: "Stop it. Y'all quit playing! Quit playing! I didn't do this stuff! This is not me! I'm fighting for my f***ing life!"

Kelly was asked a simple "yes" or "no" question—and his response was anything but simple. If you pull up the video online and watch for just a couple of minutes, you'll see exactly what I mean. His gestures are exaggerated, his emotions shift wildly, and none of it seems to flow naturally. Before the outburst, he even asked Gayle King which camera was recording—as if he needed to know where to aim his performance. That's often a sign that the truth isn't on someone's side. I've witnessed this play out in interviews countless times. The person will start crying or yelling, then suddenly glance over at me to see if I'm buying it—checking whether their act is working.

Cautionary Case Study: Amanda Knox

Amanda Knox, an American who was studying abroad in Italy, engaged in behavior that raised suspicions about her potential involvement in the murder of her roommate, Meredith Kercher. After being informed of her roommate's gruesome death, Knox was observed displaying affectionate behavior with her boyfriend, Raffaele Sollecito, at the crime scene. Investigators saw Knox's behavior as a red flag and it became a significant consideration in making her the prime suspect. Despite her arrest, she was later acquitted due to DNA evidence convicting another individual.

It is essential to recognize that human reactions to trauma and grief can vary significantly. While the inappropriate emotion can be a red flag indicating potential deceit, it is not a definitive indicator. People grieve and respond to stress in diverse ways, and what might seem like inappropriate behavior to some may be a coping mechanism for others. Therefore, while such emotional inconsistencies are noteworthy, they should be considered alongside other evidence rather than as sole indicators of guilt.

Similarly, just as emotional expressions can be misleading if viewed in isolation, so too can verbal responses—particularly when they blend truth with deception. Inserting truthful information into a lie is another common tactic.

I—INSERTING TRUTHFUL INFORMATION INTO A LIE

Due to the spotlight effect and the desire to avoid triggering a fight-or-flight response, people often include elements of the truth in their answers. This strategy helps them manage stress and avoid an adrenaline dump. Bob Costas's television interview with former Penn State Assistant Football Coach Jerry Sandusky is an example of this. Sandusky had been accused of sexually assaulting multiple juveniles on the premises of Penn State University during events for his charity, The Second Mile, which was founded to help at-risk youth.

Costas: Are you a pedophile?

Sandusky: No.

Costas: Are you sexually attracted to young boys, to underage boys?

Sandusky: Am I sexually attracted to underage boys? Sexually attracted, you know, I enjoy young people. I love to be around them. But no.

Sandusky invoked the first rule of DECEIVES by delaying—repeating the question to stall. Then he inserted several truthful statements into his lies.

"I enjoy young people."

"I love to be around them."

These statements are not criminal and serve to stall Sandusky's fight-or-flight response. Once again, think, "Did they answer your question?" Sandusky answered the question regarding whether he was a pedophile with a "no." He has rationalized that he is not a pedophile, which is a clinical term. Costas did an excellent job of following up by asking the same question differently: "Are you sexually attracted to underage boys?" The cognitive load and the spotlight effect caused Sandusky to answer deceptively. In 2012, Sandusky was found guilty on 45 counts of child sexual abuse and was sentenced to 30 to 60 years in prison.

Another example of this behavior can be seen in a conversation with parents and their college-aged child. Suppose the discussion involves the child's drinking habits. When you ask about their evening, they might say, "I had a few beers." The issue is that "a few" is subjective—it could mean two or twelve beers. Moreover, "I had a few beers" might be technically accurate, but it doesn't necessarily disclose any additional drinks consumed.

To dig deeper and gain clarity, a more effective line of questioning could go as follows:

Parent: Did you drink any alcohol last night?

Child: I had a few beers.

Parent: How many beers did you have?

Child: Five or six.

Parent: What else did you have besides beer? (Assumptive Question)

Child: I also had two vodka tonics.

The initial truth of "a few beers" can serve as a smokescreen, making it easier to obscure the full reality. As an interviewer, parent, or investigator, your task is to listen for these partial truths—and then probe beyond them.

Another example of this behavior can be observed when discussing your child's schoolwork. Imagine you ask, "Did you finish all your homework?" and your child responds, "I finished all my math homework." While this answer might seem reassuring, it may not be the whole picture. Deceptive people often provide overly specific responses. Your original question referred to *all* homework, but their answer only addressed math.

To gain clarity, you could follow up with more targeted questions:

Parent: Did you complete all your homework today?

Child: Yes, I finished my math homework.

Parent: Did you complete the homework for every subject?

Child: Well, I still have some English left.

By asking precise follow-up questions, you can reveal any gaps in the initial response, ensuring you get the complete story without leaving room for misinterpretation or incomplete work. This approach highlights the importance of asking precise follow-up questions to clarify potentially vague or incomplete answers. In addition to carefully crafted verbal answers, it's equally important to look for mismatches between what is said and how it is said—leading us to the next key concept: verbal/nonverbal disconnect.

V—VERBAL/NONVERBAL DISCONNECT

Verbal/nonverbal disconnect occurs when someone provides a verbal answer that directly contradicts their nonverbal reaction. I commonly observe this in two distinct manifestations. First, I ask a closed-ended question, and the subject answers "no" while subconsciously nodding "yes." Try it yourself: Nod your head "yes" and say the word "no." It feels unnatural. When this happens during a conversation, it should not be ignored.

Another way this disconnect appears is when someone provides a definitive answer—either "yes" or "no"—and immediately follows it with a nonverbal shoulder shrug. This incongruence should be noted. The shoulder shrug can occur on both sides or, in many situations, just one side. They might say "yes" or "no" verbally to express confidence but pair it with a single or double-sided shoulder shrug, indicating uncertainty. This usually prompts me to follow up with a clarifying question like, "Are you sure about that?" However, I am careful not to mention that I observed their contradictory behavior to the subject. Revealing this observation would provide a reason for the subject to suppress this "tell" in future interactions. It's similar to a poker player who never reveals what they identify as an opponent's "tell" during a game or tournament.

A well-known case illustrating this phenomenon is when Katie Couric spoke to former Major League Baseball player Alex Rodriguez. At the time, many baseball players were being accused of using performance-enhancing substances, prompting Couric's interview.

Couric: "For the record, have you ever used steroids, human growth hormone, or any other performance-enhancing substance?"

Rodriguez: "No."

Rodriguez nodded his head "yes" while saying "no," revealing the truth. He had practiced the questions and his responses many times before the interaction, but he couldn't prepare for his nonverbal cues betraying him.

While verbal/nonverbal disconnect reveals internal uncertainty or conflict during an answer, some individuals take a different route entirely—they evade the question altogether.

E—EVADING

When asked a closed-ended question, a straightforward "yes" or "no" response should be provided promptly. After receiving the answer, it is crucial to evaluate whether the question was truly answered or if evasion was used.

For example, a hiring manager might ask:

Q: “Have you ever committed a serious crime?”

A: “I have never been arrested!”

Or:

Q: “Have you ever committed a serious crime?”

A: “I have never been convicted!”

While these responses may technically be accurate, they could indicate that the individual has committed or been arrested for a serious crime but was never caught or convicted, as it avoids directly addressing the question.

Another example from a common applicant interaction:

Q: “Have you ever used any illegal drugs?”

A: “I don’t hang around drug users!”

This answer evades the question. While it may be true that the individual doesn’t associate with drug users, it doesn’t address whether they have personally used illegal drugs, which is often crucial for assessment.

Another common scenario:

Q: “Did you falsify any information on your application forms?”

A: “Everything I put down on that form is accurate!”

People who respond this way may be honest about what they chose to include on the form, but the issue may lie in what they omitted, thus potentially withholding relevant information.

Here are a couple of examples an HR manager might encounter in dealing with an employee accused of inappropriate behavior at work:

> **Q:** "Have you ever engaged in harassment or inappropriate workplace behavior?"
>
> **A:** "I get along with all my coworkers and have never had any complaints."

This response focuses on positive relationships and the absence of complaints without directly denying any involvement in harassment or inappropriate behavior, potentially evading the core issue. He is essentially saying that he has never been caught.

> **Q:** "Have you ever been disciplined at work for inappropriate behavior?"
>
> **A:** "I believe in maintaining professionalism and have always tried to get along with my colleagues."

Here, the employee emphasizes professionalism and good relationships but does not directly answer whether they have been disciplined, potentially avoiding disclosing past incidents.

In this final example, we look at a loan officer talking to a prospective applicant:

> **Q:** "Do you have any outstanding debts not listed on this application?"
>
> **A:** "I manage my finances responsibly and pay my bills on time."

The applicant's response highlights financial responsibility and timely bill payments but does not directly confirm the absence of unlisted debts, possibly obscuring complete financial disclosure.

In each case, the provided answers either fail to address the question directly or shift the focus away from potentially incriminating information. Recognizing these evasive tactics and asking follow-up questions to clarify and obtain truthful responses is essential. The key is always to ask yourself: Did they answer the question?

Commitment Issues as a Form of Evasion

Commitment issues, another form of evasion, manifest when individuals avoid unequivocal commitment to their statements. This reluctance stems from a fear of repercussions if their statements are later challenged. When people refrain from acknowledging their words straightforwardly, it serves as a protective measure, allowing them to hedge their responses and mitigate the psychological burden of deceit. Technically, these responses do not constitute direct lies. For example, if you inquire about someone making a specific statement to another person, and their response falls into the following categories instead of a simple "yes" or "no," it indicates a hesitancy to commit fully:

- "You could say that."
- "Don't hold me to this, but . . ."
- "As I told the other officer . . ."
- "To the best of my knowledge."
- "It's possible."

These nuanced responses reflect a certain hesitancy or unwillingness to firmly stand behind their words, potentially indicative of a reluctance to commit fully. One might consider these as attempts to give themselves some "wiggle room" later in the conversation.

Projection as a Form of Evasion

Another form of evasion is projection, which involves attributing undesirable thoughts, feelings, or traits to someone else. Often, people unconsciously deny their actions and externalize them to others.

In a child exploitation investigation in South Carolina, an individual traveled from out of state to meet an undercover police officer posing as a 13-year-old girl. During the initial interview, the suspect claimed he was traveling solely to educate the girl about the dangers of online predators. A polygraph examination was conducted to ascertain whether he had engaged in child exploitation. When I posed a straightforward yes or no question about prior victimization of a minor, the suspect responded with, "Only a monster would do something like that," and "I can't even imagine how someone could be so sick!" This response evaded the actual question and raised significant red flags. Subsequently, the suspect failed the polygraph, leading to his admission of having exploited two other minors, resulting in his arrest.

Some other common examples that illustrate this principle are the following:

Q: "Have you been cheating on me?"

A: "Why would you even ask that? You're the one who's always talking to other people and dressing provocatively."

The respondent deflects the question by accusing the questioner of similar behavior, avoiding a direct answer.

Q: "Did you cheat on the exam?"

A: "You should be asking that question to half the class; they're the ones who always cheat."

The individual projects cheating behavior onto the class, avoiding a personal admission.

Q: "Have you been using the company's printer for personal use?"

A: "Why are you talking to me about that? I saw John printing flyers for his son's Boy Scout meeting yesterday."

The individual avoids addressing their misuse of company resources by accusing another coworker of similar behavior.

In each example, the individual uses projection to avoid directly answering a yes or no question, often by deflecting the issue onto someone else or suggesting that the behavior in question is shared among others. This tactic shifts the focus away from the individual's actions and onto others, avoiding personal accountability.

Omission as a Form of Evasion

According to research, most lies told in daily life are not outright fabrications—they're omissions. In other words, people often deceive by editing the truth rather than inventing a new version of it. They share a version that is technically accurate but strategically incomplete.[13]

Open-ended prompts like "Tell me what happened" or "What did you do today" give the speaker full control over what they choose to include—and, more importantly, what they choose to leave out. This freedom creates fertile ground for deceptive omission. When individuals control the narrative, they are more likely to curate responses that serve their interests—whether to evade, protect, manipulate, or maintain a favorable image.

Fortunately, there are subtle linguistic and psychological indicators that can increase your chances of spotting potential omissions in open statements.

- **Lack of Personal Pronouns:** Omission often reveals itself through distancing language. For example, "Went out. Got gas. Came back," avoids ownership. A truth-teller is likelier to say, "I went out, gassed up the car, and then I came back home."
- **Chronological Gaps:** When the timeline jumps abruptly or a span of time is vaguely summarized—such as "We drove around town for a while, and then I went home"—that ambiguity can conceal risky behavior or omitted actions prior to coming home.

- **Qualifying Phrases:** Words and phrases like "kinda," "sort of," or "as far as I remember" may signal hedging within an open dialogue. These softeners often precede partial truths or are used to avoid full disclosure.

From a cognitive standpoint, lying by omission is easier than lying by commission. Creating a false narrative requires more mental energy—it must be constructed, maintained, and recalled consistently. In contrast, with omission, the speaker merely avoids certain details, which places less strain on memory and reduces the likelihood of being caught. This makes omission feel safer and allows deceptive individuals to remain composed and emotionally regulated.[14]

How to Respond When You Suspect Omission

When you detect potential gaps, your goal isn't to confront—it's to clarify. Reflect on moments that feel vague and invite the speaker to elaborate. Use gentle, open-ended prompts that signal curiosity rather than accusation.

- "Tell me more about that part."
- "What happened just before that?"
- "How long were you there?"

These questions provide the speaker with an opportunity to fill in blanks. Often, the details that emerge either reveal the omitted information or expose inconsistencies that warrant further inquiry.

Tightening the Leash: How to Rein In a Tall Tale

Earlier in the book, I discussed what happens when a subject can roam freely with their story; they are the proverbial "dog off the leash." At some point, especially as the story stretches credibility, you need to tighten that leash.

One of the simplest and most effective ways to do this is by switching from open-ended questions to closed-ended ones. It's a conversational gear shift that signals the need to move from exploration to clarification.

Let's say a coworker boasts about hitting 40 home runs during their senior year of high school baseball. Based on everything you know about them, that claim seems suspect. Rather than calling them out directly, you redirect with a confirming question:

"Wow, you hit 40 home runs in one season?"

Now they're boxed in. That question demands a "yes" or "no." The moment they're forced to commit, the narrative often shifts:

"Well . . . maybe not 40. I don't remember exactly. It was a lot, though."

That's the walk-back. They were free to embellish when the conversation was wide open, but with the leash tightened and a binary question on the table, they often soften their claim or quietly retreat from it. This subtle shift from open to closed questions doesn't just interrupt deception; it invites clarity and provides them an off-ramp from a potentially unsustainable lie. This tactic is particularly useful when you sense you're being misled but don't want to provoke defensiveness. It preserves rapport while subtly testing credibility.

Once you've narrowed the question and invited clarity, it's equally important to listen for how the response is delivered—because deception often leaks out through vocal inflection and tone before it does through content.

S—SHIFTING VOCAL INFLECTION: HOW SPEECH PATTERNS REVEAL DECEPTION

Changes in vocal tone, pitch, and speech patterns can provide critical indicators of deception. Studies show that when individuals lie, their vocal characteristics often shift due to increased cognitive load. These shifts include a rising inflection at the end of statements and a higher pitch when lying, which can serve as red flags for investigators, interviewers, and even the general public.

Upward Inflection at the End of a Statement ("Questioning Tone")

When people tell the truth, they typically speak confidently, using a steady and clear tone. However, when someone is lying, they may unknowingly raise the pitch of their voice at the end of a sentence, making a statement sound more like a question than a firm declaration. This vocal pattern indicates a lack of commitment to the statement and should be considered a red flag.

A truthful statement—"I didn't take the money"—will be delivered with a firm, declarative tone. A potentially deceptive response—"I didn't take the money?"—will be delivered with a subtle questioning tone, seeking validation rather than asserting the truth.

This phenomenon is especially noticeable in high-pressure situations where individuals fabricate details on the spot. Research indicates that people who believe in their innocence tend to speak in firm, declarative tones, while those who are deceptive often exhibit vocal uncertainty by raising their pitch at the end of their statements.

Increased Pitch When Lying

Lying is mentally taxing. A deceptive person must create a false narrative, recall previous lies, and observe the listener's reactions—all while suppressing anxiety. This increased cognitive load and stress response can lead to an involuntary rise in vocal pitch, a physiological response to sympathetic nervous system activation. Upward inflection in response to direct questioning should trigger additional follow-up questions. Individuals who believe they are innocent typically speak with certainty, steering clear of question-like tones in their denials.[15]

In a post-trial interview, when asked directly whether he killed Nicole Brown Simpson, O. J. Simpson responded with: "I would never do that? I mean, I loved her?"

The upward inflection in "I would never do that?" sounded more like a question than a denial. This vocal uncertainty stood in stark contrast to his usual confident speaking style.

Case Example: When Vocal Inflection Revealed the Truth

In a particularly disturbing case in Missouri, a suspect's vocal shifts revealed the full extent of his crimes. The subject had already admitted to a criminal act against a minor following a polygraph examination. However, when asked if there were any additional victims, his voice inflection betrayed him before his words did. His response was, "Noooooo?"—the drawn-out, upward pitch at the end made it sound like a hesitant question rather than a firm denial. Almost immediately after, he followed up with "Whyyyy?"—a classic stalling tactic to regain control of the conversation. During follow-up questioning, the suspect eventually admitted to an additional victim.

SOMETIMES YOU MUST EMBRACE THE LIE

I always stress in my training that my trainees must be flexible in their approach during interviews. Sometimes, we may not obtain a full confession; instead, we might get admissions. If admissions are impossible, we aim for intelligence that can be leveraged in future interactions with other subjects. When actionable intelligence is not forthcoming, we strive to build future goodwill and cooperation.

It is not only acceptable but necessary in some circumstances to allow someone to lie to you during an interview. In certain situations, this is a deliberate tactic. Rather than immediately challenging inconsistencies or confronting the subject with evidence, it is often much more productive to let them walk through their version of events uninterrupted.

By withholding what you know, you prevent the subject from shaping their story to fit the disclosed facts. The moment you share information—even subtly—you provide them the chance to adjust their narrative, making it much more difficult to expose deception later on. Enabling the subject to express themselves freely serves a crucial purpose: It generates inconsistencies that you can later test and address at the most opportune moment.

Here's a case in point. In the investigation of an armed robbery, detectives captured doorbell camera footage of the main suspect arriving at a friend's apartment in the early afternoon on the day of the crime. Intelligence suggested that he obtained the firearm used in the incident during this visit. When questioned later, the suspect denied participating in the robbery and ultimately consented to a polygraph test.

During that examination, I intentionally chose not to mention the footage or our suspicions about the firearm. I wanted to hear how he would explain his movements—without the advantage of knowing what we already knew.

Me: "Help me out here. Can you walk me through what you did yesterday?"

Subject: "Yesterday, (pause) ummm, I was home all day playing Xbox."

Me: "What were you playing?"

Subject: "Call of Duty."

Me: "You play against people online?"

Subject: "That's the only way to play. I hate the dumb story mode."

Me: "Did you get a chance to get out of the house at all?"

Subject: "I went and got some gas around eight."

Me: "Where did you gas up?"

Subject: "The Citgo station down the street."

By resisting the urge to confront this falsehood, I allowed him to entrench himself in a narrative that could later be disproved. His Xbox was forensically examined, and a subpoena was sent to Microsoft for online play records. Surveillance footage from the Citgo station was also reviewed to confirm he was not there at 8 p.m. Although the suspect never confessed to the robbery, the lies he provided, combined with the evidence collected by the police department, secured a conviction.

Had I revealed the existence of the doorbell camera footage too soon, the suspect could have easily adjusted his narrative: "Oh, I stopped by John's real quick to grab a beer, then went home." By doing so, we would have lost a valuable inconsistency and key leverage with it.

Even if a complete confession isn't achieved, obtaining verifiable falsehoods is an immensely beneficial result. These falsehoods enable you to challenge the individual's credibility, illustrate a motive to mislead, and offer significant leverage during the interview or in court proceedings. In short, sometimes the smartest move is to make no move at all. Let them talk. Let them lie. Let them build a narrative that cannot withstand the evidence you've kept in reserve.

Another illustration of this principle occurred in a homicide case in Texas. Authorities found the suspect at a flea market, where he was selling an antique double-barreled shotgun that had been stolen from the home of a missing elderly woman. This evidence quickly placed him on the list of suspects—and the prior information about him working on the missing woman's farm made him the prime suspect. He was taken into custody under suspicion of abducting and murdering the woman, who was a well-respected member of her local community.

Initially, the suspect denied any involvement, claiming he had purchased the stolen shotgun from a stranger at a gas station. Although the story was implausible, he remained steadfast in his refusal to confess. However, he did agree to take a polygraph examination with us—my partner Brian Luley and me.

When the suspect failed the polygraph, we quickly adjusted our goals for the interview. While we had initially hoped for a full confession—one that would reveal both his role in the crime and the location of the woman's body—we recognized that securing an outright admission of murdering a beloved member of the community posed an immense psychological barrier. The likelihood of a full confession was slim.

We changed our focus toward a more attainable goal: recovering the victim's body. If the suspect led us to the body, it would demonstrate guilty knowledge and establish probable cause for a murder charge, while allowing the Texas Department of Public Safety's world-class forensics unit to work backward and gather additional evidence.

In shifting tactics, we aimed to lessen the weight of the admission on his conscience, suggesting that perhaps the crime hadn't been entirely his idea. At this point, the suspect's body language and demeanor changed significantly. Over the next four hours, he spun an elaborate story about how he had accompanied a friend who had planned the burglary.

We pressed for precise details about this alleged accomplice, knowing the story was fabricated. Our strategy was to gather as much information as possible to later disprove the existence of this imaginary third party—providing provable lies that would further damage his credibility if the case proceeded to trial.

At this stage, we shifted the tone of the conversation to appeal to the suspect's remaining sense of humanity. We explained that our primary goal was to help bring closure to the victim's family. Moved by this, the suspect asked to pray with us. Brian facilitated the prayer, after which the suspect agreed to lead us to an abandoned farmhouse where he had disposed of the woman's body.

Ultimately, the suspect was convicted of murder and sentenced to life in prison. His decision to lead us to the body—a location only the guilty party could have known—and the verifiable lies he had told about the fictitious accomplice sealed the case.

Across these cases, a consistent theme emerges: the words people choose, and how they deliver them, often betray what they're trying to conceal. This is where Behavioral Indicator Questions can provide an additional tool during verbal interactions.

CHAPTER 13

Behavioral Indicator Questions (BIQs)

"Better to remain silent and be thought a fool
than to speak and remove all doubt."
—Abraham Lincoln

During difficult conversations, silence can be revealing—but even more so are the words people choose when they do speak. A well-placed question, framed correctly, doesn't just prompt a response; it reveals how a person thinks, rationalizes, and reacts under pressure.

Throughout my career, I've relied on a core set of Behavioral Indicator Questions (BIQs)—well-crafted prompts that reveal deception by evaluating both verbal and behavioral responses. Variations of these questions have been utilized in law enforcement and corporate investigations for over 50 years, but I've refined my technique based on real-world experience in high-stakes interviews.

Unlike traditional interrogation methods that rely on accusation and confrontation, BIQs work by subtly inviting individuals to disclose information without realizing they are doing so. How someone answers—or struggles to answer—often tells us far more than the content of their words.[1] The following questions are some of the most common ones I utilize during investigative interviews.

- What are three reasons someone would do something like this?
- What do you think should happen to the person who did this?
- Is there any reason why [your DNA, fingerprints, surveillance footage, cell phone records] would show you were involved in this situation?
- Why should I believe you?

This chapter will explore each of these questions in more detail and examine some common, everyday applications.

BIQ QUESTION #1: WHAT ARE THREE REASONS SOMEONE WOULD DO SOMETHING LIKE THIS?

The first question leverages the principles of availability bias and recency bias. Memories in the brain are like files in a cabinet, with the most recent or significant ones at the front. By asking this question, I tap into the subject's recent or prominent thoughts.

In my experience over thousands of interviews, I have found that individuals who later confessed to criminal activity often gave me a "preview" of their reasons and rationalizations when they answered this question. This question provides insight into the criminal decision-making process and may give the suspect (unconsciously) the opportunity to provide helpful context to what really happened.

When asked to explain why *someone* might commit a crime, suspects often project their own motivations without realizing it. This is due to availability bias—the psychological tendency to pull from personal experiences when answering hypothetical questions. Guilty individuals unknowingly list reasons they themselves have considered or acted upon.

Innocent individuals usually provide more generic answers or struggle to generate meaningful responses.

In a homicide case involving a young girl killed by a stray bullet, I asked the suspect a strategic question: "What are three reasons someone might shoot another person?" He replied, "Disrespect, gang activity, and maybe the person was showing off guns." Later in the interview, the suspect confessed to firing at rival gang members after they saw him showing off his assault rifle. His earlier answers gave me invaluable insight into his mindset on that evening of the shooting. That insight shaped the way I approached him during our later conversation, paving the way to his confession. It worked much like a social media algorithm—his previous input helped guide my next move, making each step in the conversation more relevant and effective.

In another gang-related homicide investigation in the Midwest, I asked the suspect his three reasons for why someone would shoot another person. His answer was, "Revenge, disrespect, and retaliation for hurting a friend." He later confessed to me that he killed the rival gang member to enact revenge after the victim shot his friend. He had provided the motive for the killing unconsciously by answering the three reasons question. The suspect was subsequently convicted of murder and sentenced to over 30 years in prison.

Of course, this question also has many applications beyond criminal investigations. Imagine that a hypothetical corporate investigation led the employee to state the following:

Q: "What do you think are three reasons someone would embezzle company funds?"

A: "Well, someone might do this because they are struggling financially, feel underappreciated at work, or maybe they don't think they will get caught."

If I were to utilize themes to obtain admissions from this employee, I would focus on their current financial situation, lack of appreciation at work, and the poor security that made them think they would not get caught.

This behavioral question effectively probes the respondent's mindset and motivations. The interviewer often uncovers the respondent's thought processes and justifications by encouraging suspects to speculate on why someone might commit a crime. The technique leverages cognitive biases, such as availability bias, where the most readily available thoughts or recent experiences influence the suspect's answers. This method is particularly effective in highlighting unconscious admissions of guilt, as respondents frequently project their own motives onto hypothetical perpetrators. But potential motives are only part of the picture. To get an even clearer sense of guilt or innocence, I turn to the next key question: *What do you think should happen to the person who did this?*

BIQ #2: "WHAT DO YOU THINK SHOULD HAPPEN TO THE PERSON WHO DID THIS?"

This question engages moral reasoning and self-projection. People instinctively assess wrongdoing based on their personal experiences, biases, and level of involvement. Individuals with guilt often soften their views on punishment because, consciously or unconsciously, they are judging themselves. They tend to downplay punishment, offering more lenient or ambiguous consequences (e.g., "Everyone deserves a second chance" or "They should get help"). This serves as a defense mechanism to diminish the seriousness of their actions. In contrast, innocent individuals typically propose firm, socially acceptable consequences without hesitation. They exhibit strong moral clarity, often suggesting severe consequences that align with societal norms (e.g., "They should go to jail" or "They should be fired").

In cases involving the potential for serious punishment, guilty individuals are more likely to recommend treatment rather than punishment—rationalizing their behavior as something that can be "fixed" instead of condemned.[2]

In a murder investigation, I asked a suspect what should happen to someone who killed an innocent child in a drive-by shooting. His response?

"Well, everyone deserves a second chance."

That statement alone didn't prove guilt, but it was a red flag. A neutral or innocent person would typically respond with outrage—something like, "They should go to prison for life" or "Whoever did that is a monster." The suspect's hesitation to condemn the act suggested he was evaluating the punishment in relation to himself—and sure enough, after failing a polygraph, he confessed.

In the context of an internal theft investigation, when responding to the punishment question—"What do you think should happen to someone who embezzles $500,000?"—an innocent individual typically advocates strong punishment, such as termination or legal action, reflecting a clear stance against misconduct. Conversely, a suggestion like "they should pay the money back" may indicate a more lenient perspective, which *could* be associated with deceptive behavior since those consequences would be applied to them if they were the guilty party.

However, it's crucial to approach such interpretations with caution. Not all lenient responses indicate guilt; cultural or personal beliefs, or a peaceful disposition, might influence an individual's opinion on appropriate disciplinary measures. Therefore, while the punishment question can be valuable in assessing credibility, responses to it should be considered alongside other behavioral cues and evidence to form a comprehensive evaluation.

BIQ QUESTION 3: IS THERE ANY REASON WHY?

This question forces the subject to mentally confront potential evidence before they know what you actually have. Innocent people have no reason to hedge their answer—they confidently say "no" because they know they weren't there. Guilty individuals, however, often adjust their story to account for possible evidence.

Asking this question leverages cognitive dissonance—the discomfort that arises when a person's internal knowledge (their guilt) conflicts with what they are saying. To manage this discomfort, deceptive individuals often modify their denials, shifting from outright rejection to partial admissions as they prepare for the possibility of being caught. Guilty individuals hedge their response with uncertainty ("I don't think so" or "Not that I know of") or gradually modify their answer as they try to manage the risk of being caught. Truthful individuals provide an immediate, unqualified "no" without hesitation.

In a homicide investigation, I spoke to a suspect who was adamant that he was on the other side of town during the shooting. I told him the police department was about to obtain a subpoena for his cell phone GPS data and asked him whether it would place him at the scene of the shooting. His response:

"Ummm, I don't think so."

That raised an immediate red flag. If he was certain he was on the other side of town when previously asked about his whereabouts, this new hypothetical question should not have caused such hesitation and uncertainty. He should have answered "no" in a timely fashion. This suggested he was considering what data might exist before committing to an answer. Over time, his responses evolved from "I don't think so" to "It's possible" and finally to "Yes, I was there."

In another homicide I worked, the individual said he could not have killed the other person two days prior because he hadn't shot a gun in over a year. I had little additional evidence to use, so I posed a question.

Me: "So, sometimes in cases like this, the police department is able to utilize a gunshot residue test. It can pick up microscopic traces of gunshot residue that stick to people's skin after they shoot a gun. These wipes can sometimes test positive if you have discharged a gun in the last seven days. Is there any reason this test would show you shot a gun in the last seven days?"

Suspect: "Um. You know . . . now that I think about it, we did some target practice about a week ago."

Me: "Okay, thanks for sharing. That's important to know."

Me: "Was it at a local range?"

Suspect: "Nah. It was way out in the country."

Me: "What type of location?"

Suspect: "Just some dude's farm."

Me: "Was it a friend of yours?"

Suspect: "Uhh. Not really. It was just a friend of a friend kinda thing."

Me: "What kind of guns did you guys shoot?"

Suspect: "I can't really remember."

Now, at this point, I think any reader can see that the subject is not being truthful. He is trying to get out in front of the fact that he is afraid of the mythical gunshot residue test. As a result, he is forced to begin constructing a story. This eventually led to a conversation in which he confessed to shooting the assault rifle that killed an 11-year-old girl. He was subsequently convicted of murder and sentenced to over 40 years in prison.

Another example of the effectiveness of these Behavioral Indicator Questions occurred when my partner Brian and I assisted a local police department with an arson/homicide investigation. The medical examiner stated that the deceased female appeared to have been strangled to death before a fire was set in the apartment (in an apparent attempt to conceal evidence). The preliminary investigation identified several people of interest. One of the suspects had received a call from the murder victim about an hour before her death.

During our interview, the suspect stated he had not left his residence that night. At this point, I explained to him that many resources were being utilized in this investigation due to the entire apartment complex almost being burned down during the incident. I asked the suspect a specific behavioral analysis question because his residence was only a few blocks from the victim's apartment. I asked him if he was familiar with the bank next to the victim's apartment complex. He stated, "Yes." I explained that they had fantastic surveillance footage due to the bank being FDIC-insured. I said they were probably in the process of requesting the footage and then asked, "Is there any reason whatsoever that footage will show you walking by the bank at three thirty in the morning?" The suspect took a long pause, then a deep breath, and assumed a confession posture. He admitted to my partner and me that he had strangled the victim after an argument and set the fire to cover his tracks. He was subsequently convicted of murder and sentenced to life in prison.

When I'm still unsure about someone's honesty—perhaps they've shown multiple behavioral indicators of deception or given vague, delayed answers—I turn to one of the simplest yet most revealing questions: "Why should I believe you?"

BIQ QUESTION #4: WHY SHOULD I BELIEVE YOU?

I learned this technique from former FBI Special Agent Jack Schafer. Following a conversation with an individual in which I have doubts about their honesty, I might ask the following: "John, I understand your point of view. Why should I believe you?" A truthful person *should* quickly respond with a variation of "because I am telling you the truth." Any response involving projection or rationalization, such as "Why would I lie?" or "I'm not that type of person," or "What do you mean?" *should* be considered a red flag.[3]

WATCH

We've explored the core principles of detecting deception and introduced behavioral assessment questions as key tools. To help trainees evaluate whether a subject has been truthful during an interview, I teach a practical framework summarized by the acronym WATCH. This method guides you on what to do after posing a close-ended or yes/no question:

- **W:** Wait briefly after asking the question.
  Allow a brief pause for the subject to respond naturally, without interruption.
- **A:** Assess verbal and nonverbal behavior.
  Consider the subject's words, tone, and body language to gather valuable data.
- **T:** Take note of deviations from the baseline.
  Watch for behaviors that diverge from the subject's established patterns.
- **C:** Check for clusters of red flags.
  Focus on identifying multiple signs of inconsistency rather than isolated anomalies.
- **H:** Highlight areas for follow-up.
  Mark specific behaviors or responses that require further questioning or clarification.

By applying the WATCH framework, you're enhancing your ability to detect potential dishonesty and creating an environment where subjects can clarify inconsistencies or reconsider whether being deceptive is in their best interest. Sometimes, the other person may misunderstand the question or feel anxious about a specific topic. In my experience conducting hundreds of pre-employment polygraph examinations, I often observed behavioral clusters that deviated from the subject's baseline established from watching them answer questions earlier during the interview. When that happened, I didn't jump to conclusions. Instead, I would ask simple, open-ended questions like, "Did that question bring something specific to mind?" or "Do you need any clarification on that question?"

This approach frequently led to admissions, but just as often, it opened the door to meaningful conversations where I could clarify the question's intent. In many cases, this helped eliminate doubts or inconsistencies, allowing the subject to complete the polygraph successfully.

By listening carefully and applying these principles, you can foster a setting where subjects feel comfortable enough to tell the truth and ensure you gather accurate and reliable information.

PUTTING IT ALL TOGETHER

Imagine a scenario in which a manager at a company has received information that leads them to believe that one of their employees has accessed restricted company files without authorization. This company has large amounts of proprietary technology, and these files could have immense value to another company. The manager calls the employee in for an interview and assesses the employee's credibility by using BIQs and analyzing their responses using the DECEIVES protocol.

Manager: "What are three reasons someone might access restricted files without authorization?"

Truthful response: "Maybe they made a mistake, had permission but used the wrong login, or were trying to help someone who didn't have access."

- Provides clear, neutral explanations.
- Does not personally project motives.

Deceptive response: "Uh . . . well, maybe they were just curious, or, um, trying to help someone, or, you know, they needed the information for something important."

- Hesitates before answering.
- Justifies the action rather than giving neutral possibilities.
- Struggles to complete the list and uses vague wording.

Manager: "What do you think should happen to someone who accesses these files without permission?"

Truthful response: "If it was an accident, they should get a warning. But if they did it intentionally, there should be consequences—maybe suspension or termination."

- Provides a balanced, logical response.
- Differentiates between accidental and intentional actions.

Deceptive response: "I mean . . . if they didn't do anything harmful, I don't think it's a big deal. Maybe just tell them not to do it again?"

- Minimizes the seriousness of the situation.
- Uses qualifiers like "if they didn't do anything harmful" to downplay the offense.
- Avoids suggesting real consequences.

Manager: "Is there any reason why the IT records would show you accessed those files?"

Truthful response: "No, I never accessed them."

- Denies the action immediately and firmly.
- Does not add unnecessary explanations.

Deceptive response: "Uh . . . I mean, I might have logged in, but I wasn't actually reading those files."

- Hesitates and hedges before answering.
- Admits partial truth while trying to control the narrative.
- Displays discomfort, such as shifting posture or avoiding eye contact.

Manager: "Why should I believe you?"

Truthful response: "Because I'm telling the truth. You can check the logs—I wasn't in those files."

- Direct, straightforward answer.
- Offers verifiable proof.

Deceptive response: "Why are you even asking me this? I've worked here for years! I would never do something like that."

- Deflects and challenges the legitimacy of the question.
- Avoids directly denying the accusation.
- Overcompensates with personal credibility rather than evidence.

From Detection to Disclosure

The manager gains valuable insight into the employee's honesty by structuring an inquiry around BIQs and utilizing DECEIVES to evaluate responses. The deceptive employee inadvertently reveals uncertainty and discomfort, making it easier to identify inconsistencies. This method, applicable in corporate settings, investigations, and personal conversations, helps uncover the truth when someone may be attempting to conceal it.

The ability to detect deception is only half the battle. Once inconsistencies are identified, the next challenge is guiding the individual toward telling the truth. People rarely confess outright—admissions are a process, not a moment. By understanding how to lower resistance, provide an "out," and structure conversations effectively, you can move from suspicion to disclosure.

Before we explore the techniques for guiding someone toward disclosure, it's essential to understand what the research shows about false confessions—and how to safeguard against them. Ethical interviewing isn't just about gaining admissions; it's about ensuring those admissions are reliable and free from coercion.

Building Trustworthy Admissions: Safeguards Against False Confessions

As shown in previous cases and methods that will be discussed in later chapters, well-conducted interviews can result in important admissions. However, it is just as critical to protect against the risk of false confessions.

Throughout my career, I have developed a clear set of principles to ensure that any admission I obtain is both truthful and reliable. An unreliable confession is worse than no confession at all. That is why I follow strict safeguards to protect both the subject and the integrity of the interview process. False confessions are rare when proper protections are in place; however, research has shown that under certain conditions, especially when those protections are absent, false confessions do occur. I take this risk seriously and actively work to mitigate it in every interview I conduct.

During my training and practice, I have implemented a number of safeguards supported by both field experience and key research on false confessions.[4,5]

- **I do not fabricate evidence.** If I lack it, I do not claim it exists. False evidence ploys are one of the most well-documented contributors to false confessions.
- **I preserve "hold-back" evidence whenever possible.** These are details of the crime known only to law enforcement and the true perpetrator. A valid confession should include facts that only the guilty party could know.
- **I never promise leniency or make guarantees.** I am extremely careful not to imply that a confession will automatically lead to a reduced sentence or favorable outcome.
- **I actively avoid prolonged interrogation.** I ensure that interviews do not run to excessive lengths, especially beyond six hours, and I provide regular breaks.
- **I do not subject individuals to sleep deprivation.** The interview is paused or rescheduled if a subject is sleep-deprived or fatigued.
- **I assess for drug use or withdrawal.** If an individual is under the influence or in withdrawal, I do not proceed with the interview until they are in a suitable physical and mental state.

- **I avoid physical discomfort.** Subjects are provided comfortable seating, reasonable room temperature, and access to food, water, and restroom breaks.
- **I am highly cautious when interviewing juveniles, individuals with mental illness, and other vulnerable populations.** I use simplified language, avoid leading questions, frequently check for comprehension, and recommend the presence of legal counsel or a parent in appropriate cases.
- **I never attempt to reconstruct a subject's memory** or suggest details they might not independently recall.
- **I maintain a calm, non-threatening demeanor throughout.** I do not raise my voice, intimidate, or threaten individuals during the interview process.
- **I advocate for and practice the recording of all interviews whenever possible.** A full recording provides transparency and allows the entire process to be dissected by investigators, legal counsel, and the court. It is one of the best modern safeguards we have to protect both the subject and the integrity of the confession.

False confessions are extremely rare when proper protocols are followed. The greater danger lies not in using themes or rapport-building but in applying any technique without adequate safeguards and professional discipline.

There is no substitute for judgment, training, and the consistent application of ethical interviewing practices. Having established a foundation of safeguards, we can now turn to one of the most practical and powerful tools for guiding subjects toward honest admissions: the ADMIT method.

CHAPTER 14

Getting them to ADMIT

"If you wish to persuade me, you must think my thoughts, feel my feelings, and speak my words."
—Cicero

The hardest part of uncovering deception isn't spotting the lie—it's getting the person to admit the truth. When you confront someone with their dishonesty, their natural instinct is to resist, deny, or rationalize their actions. This is why the best interrogators, negotiators, and communicators don't demand confessions—they guide people toward them.

Chinese military general and author of *The Art of War* Sun Tzu famously said, "When you surround an army, leave an outlet free. Do not press a desperate foe too hard." This principle isn't just for warfare—it's crucial in high-stakes conversations. When people feel trapped, they dig in. But when given a way out—a narrative that preserves their dignity—they are far more likely to acknowledge the truth.[1]

For over 25 years, I've refined a system to do exactly that. ADMIT is a structured approach that shifts the conversation from resistance to disclosure. This approach has been modified from traditional systems used by law enforcement and intelligence agencies. People tend to imagine a law enforcement interrogation wherein two police detectives grill a suspect about their involvement in a crime. We visualize the detectives yelling at the suspect or playing good cop/bad cop. These approaches are highly ineffective.

A good interview isn't about grilling—it's more similar to long, low-temperature barbecue. If you rush the process, turning up the heat too high, you burn the meat before it ever gets tender. But if you control the temperature, let the flavors develop, and give it time, the toughest cuts become soft and fall apart. Interviews work the same way. With the right preparation, patience, and environment, people open up. The key is knowing when to apply pressure and when to let things rest.

Adopting the slow-cooking philosophy of barbecue for engaging in difficult or sensitive conversations underscores that patient, methodical approaches can transform even the most challenging situations into successful outcomes, making even the toughest "meat" more palatable.

Once we determine that someone has been deceptive and we need to establish the truth, it's crucial to shift from a dialogue to a monologue. During this phase, we must control the narrative by telling our stories, which helps us manage the perceived blame and reduce the impact on the person being questioned. We create a stream of curated information, much like Facebook or Instagram reels, which captures and holds their attention.

So, what are the steps for getting the other person to ADMIT?

Step 1—A: Address the Subject's Position

Step 2—D: Disarm the Subject's Denial

Step 3—M: Manage the Discussion by using the BUDDY Technique

Step 4—I: Identify Signs of Receptivity

Step 5—T: Transition to Admission or Agreement

In this chapter, we'll explore each of these steps in detail and provide examples of how they play out in a range of interactions.

STEP 1: A—ADDRESS THE SUBJECT'S POSITION

An angler must allow a large fish to take some line using the reel's drag. However, the angler must set the hook and reel the fish at a certain point. This timing is similarly important to obtaining an admission after someone is deceptive during an interview. There comes a moment when the interviewer needs to turn the conversation into a monologue, addressing the other person in a nonconfrontational manner to elicit the truth.

A critical aspect is to avoid directly calling someone a liar. It usually results in a reflexive denial, as people instinctively want to stay consistent with their previous statements and actions. This can lead to a counterproductive back-and-forth of accusations and denials. To avoid this, the goal is to present the evidence to encourage the suspect to acknowledge their involvement without feeling attacked.

When confronting someone, it's essential to evaluate the level of evidence you have. If the evidence is overwhelming, you may handle it with a more assertive stance.

Example 1—Strong Evidence: Academic Plagiarism

Professor: "Bob, a careful review of your exam clearly shows you did not write that paper. I understand this might be difficult, but being truthful now can significantly affect how we proceed."

Example 2—Strong Evidence: Fake Bomb Threat

Interviewer: "Bob, after our discussion and my review of the facts, there is no doubt you were involved in this situation. Until now, you were the only person who knew the truth, but now we both do. I know the what and the who, but the most important thing I need to understand right now is the why."

The approach used in the last two examples helps convey certainty and confidence. By clearly and respectfully presenting the evidence, the interviewer creates an environment where the suspect feels compelled to come forward with the truth rather than becoming defensive and resistant.

When You Still Have Doubts—Evidence Not as Strong

When a subject is confronted with evidence of their involvement in a situation, their immediate verbal and nonverbal responses can reveal a lot about their culpability. My experience has been that a guilty person will typically say things that lack confidence regarding their innocence after they are confronted with a well-constructed question. I mean, put yourself in the shoes of a suspect. A detective has just accused you of committing a crime. How would you react? Think back to when you were accused of something you didn't do. It could have been an accusation from a parent, coworker, or spouse. If you didn't do it, you most likely would react with a strong denial, and that denial would remain consistent. This is the same way a truthful suspect will likely respond: with solid and direct denials and an assertive demeanor.

In these situations, I'll say something like:

"I have some issues with what you're saying to me and we need to sort this out."

"It appears you haven't been completely forthcoming with me."

In my experience, guilty individuals often display uncertainty or avoid providing a direct denial altogether. Rather than confidently rejecting the accusation, they may respond with vague, noncommittal phrases—often delivered with an upward inflection that signals doubt or surprise, such as:

"Really?"

"No kidding?"

"Seriously?"

When innocent people are accused, they *tend* to offer solid and consistent denials. Research shows that innocent individuals are *more likely* to be steadfast and unwavering in their denials because they are confident in their truth and have nothing to hide. You see how the words "tend" and "more likely" are emphasized. There are very few absolutes in lie detection. I view their lack of a strong reaction as a red flag. It is another indicator. However, we must never view it as an absolute. Patterns of behavior are the key.

Research highlights that innocent suspects are usually consistent in their narratives while maintaining their innocence despite prolonged and intense questioning. Their confidence in their innocence supports their ability to provide coherent and stable accounts.[2] Innocent individuals often show signs of genuine stress and disbelief when falsely accused, as opposed to guilty individuals who might show inappropriate levels of calmness or exaggerated distress.[3]

STEP 2: D—DISARM THE SUBJECT'S DENIALS

At this stage, whether the denial is verbal or nonverbal (such as shaking one's head, crossing arms, or shifting away), it is crucial to address these denials immediately. If not managed promptly, the interaction can turn into a back-and-forth exchange of denials, which can become adversarial and hinder the interview process. Every time a person repeats a denial, they psychologically commit to it, reinforcing their stance and making it increasingly difficult for them to reverse course. The more they deny, the harder it becomes for them to backtrack without losing credibility or feeling exposed.

The key to disarming denials is cutting them off early—before they gain momentum. Once a person gets into a rhythm of saying "I didn't do it" or "That's not true," it solidifies their resistance, making them less likely to shift their position. Instead of allowing the subject to dig themselves into a deeper hole, the interviewer must disrupt the pattern and redirect their focus.

Here are effective techniques to stop denials before they take hold.

- **Break Eye Contact:** A subtle shift in gaze can interrupt their thought process. Instead of locking eyes and reinforcing their defensiveness, briefly look away and say, "Hold on a second . . ." This small but intentional pause creates a natural disruption, stopping them mid-thought.
- **Use Their Name:** Personalization demands attention and makes the interaction feel more direct. Saying, "John, let's be honest

with each other here," applies gentle social pressure, reminding them that this is a personal conversation, not just a confrontation.

- **Use a Calming or Reassuring Tone:** Instead of sounding accusatory, soften your tone to convey that you're not looking for a fight. "Look, I get why you'd want to say that, but let's focus on what really happened." This approach keeps the conversation constructive rather than adversarial.
- **Redirect the Conversation:** Instead of engaging in a debate over their denial, guide the discussion toward something they can open up about. "I hear what you're saying, but let's focus on what really matters—what led to this situation?" By shifting the emphasis from *whether* they did something to *why* it happened, you remove the immediate threat to their ego and allow them to consider a response that doesn't feel like an outright confession.
- **Acknowledge Without Accepting:** If a denial is already in motion, acknowledge it without reinforcing it. "I understand why you'd say that," or "I hear you." This makes the person feel heard without validating their denial, keeping the door open for them to adjust their stance.

By mastering the art of cutting off denials before they snowball, you can keep the conversation fluid and guide the subject toward a more productive dialogue. The goal isn't to argue—it's to create an environment where admitting the truth feels easier than maintaining a lie.

STEP 3: M—MANAGE THE CONVERSATION BY BEING THEIR BUDDY

To increase the likelihood of someone making a disclosure, it's crucial to understand and implement these tactics. I refer to this approach as becoming their BUDDY. This strategy is vital for fostering an environment where the individual feels less defensive and more open to sharing information. Utilizing these methods can mitigate the emotional intensity associated with disclosure and promote honesty. This doesn't mean I condone their poor choices or wrongful actions; instead, I'm practicing short-term situational empathy. This involves attributing responsibility to external factors, comprehending their actions from their perspective, and minimizing the impact of their actions. Additionally, incorporating stories, analogies, and metaphors can help the person connect with the other person's viewpoint.

The BUDDY Method

- B—Blaming something or someone else for the person's actions.
- U—Understanding of the reasoning behind the other person's actions or choices.
- D—Diminishing the impact of the person's actions or choices.
- D—Developing a personalized narrative using stories, metaphors, and analogies.
- Y—"Y" is more important than "what."

How to Utilize the BUDDY Concept

Imagine you're the main advisor to President Harry S. Truman in the quiet aftermath of World War II. You are sitting with him as the weight of his decision to authorize the atomic bombings of Hiroshima and Nagasaki hangs heavy in the room. As his trusted confidant, you see him burdened by moral reflection. Here's how the BUDDY framework could guide that difficult conversation:

You: "Mr. President, I can't imagine the emotional toll you've carried. No leader should ever have to make such a decision. But let's remember—this war wasn't of your choosing. Japan's attack on Pearl Harbor forced our hand. You stepped into a storm already raging." (*Blame the situation*)

Truman: "Still . . . sometimes I wonder if there might've been another way—one less devastating."

You: "Of course you do. Any decent man would. But after the bloodshed at Iwo Jima, Okinawa, and Tarawa—where our troops faced relentless resistance—you were staring at the reality of a ground invasion that could've cost over a million lives. The enemy's willingness to fight to the last man—and even mobilize civilians—left you with no easy options." (*Understand the reasoning*)

Truman: "But those bombs . . . they didn't just target soldiers. They destroyed cities. Women. Children."

You: "Yes, and that grief is real. But consider what might have unfolded without them—a prolonged war that would've claimed even more innocent lives on both sides. Your decision, as hard as it was, brought the war to an immediate end. You shortened suffering. That matters. Sometimes the most merciful path is also the most painful one." (*Diminish the impact*)

Truman: "It still feels like a terrible burden. The destruction . . . it was absolute."

You: "It was. But, sir, imagine you were a captain steering a ship through a typhoon. You didn't summon the storm, but you had to navigate through it—knowing lives depended on you. And here's something history won't forget: You possessed the most powerful weapon the world had ever seen. You could have used it to dominate, to conquer. But you didn't. You ended the war and then showed restraint. That's not just leadership—that's character." (*Develop a narrative with metaphor*)

Truman: "You know, I hadn't looked at it quite like that before . . ."

Now, let's break down how to be someone's BUDDY in everyday situations.

(B)—Blaming Something or Someone Else for the Person's Actions

When discussing mistakes with individuals, it is essential to let them attribute their unacceptable thoughts, feelings, or actions to external factors or other people. This technique allows them to deflect personal blame and associate their actions with external influences, making it easier to admit their behavior. By casting blame onto external circumstances or other people, we can reduce the other person's internal conflict and facilitate a more open and honest dialogue. Projecting blame can alleviate another person's guilt and shame, making it easier for them to confess. People who believe factors beyond their control influence their actions are likelier to open up about their behavior.[4]

Using this technique, we can help the other person shift the blame away from their personal character. For instance, we might say, "If you were not influenced by bad company or were misled, you probably wouldn't have done this." This approach helps others see themselves as victims of circumstance, reducing internal conflict and making it easier for them to admit their actions.

In a case involving drugs, a person might say, "I understand that addiction can make people do things they wouldn't normally do. It's not entirely your fault if you were struggling with substance abuse." This statement projects the blame onto the addiction, allowing the suspect to dissociate their actions from their moral character and feel more comfortable admitting their behavior.

In a situation involving academic fraud, a principal might say to a student accused of plagiarism, "I can see how the pressure to get into college and your job after school taking up all of your free time might have led you to make these decisions. It's tough when the pressure is high, and you are overwhelmed." This empathetic projection helps the other person feel understood and less judged, making them more likely to disclose.

In an employee time fraud scenario, a manager at a large retail store may say to an employee suspected of time card fraud, "I know things have been crazy lately, especially with the extra workload everyone's been carrying during the peak holiday rush. When hammered with crazy hours, people sometimes feel they don't get enough downtime. It's easy to see how taking some extra breaks might have felt like the only way to catch your breath and get back on track. We all have moments where things feel overwhelming. Now let's talk about it."

(U)—Understanding of Reasoning Behind the Other Person's Actions or Choices

Guilt and shame are powerful barriers to disclosure. When individuals experience overwhelming guilt, they are less likely to admit to their actions due to fear of judgment and internal conflict. However, by offering logical explanations for their behavior, we can help alleviate these emotions, making it easier for them to disclose. This technique allows the individual to feel understood rather than condemned, fostering a sense of psychological safety. As discussed earlier regarding Maslow's Hierarchy of Needs, psychological safety is at the base of the pyramid and must be established to ensure disclosure.

Rationalization works by reframing actions in a more understandable and less condemnable light. It shifts the narrative away from the individual's intrinsic flaws or moral failings and toward external factors influencing their behavior. Offering plausible explanations for the person's behavior helps resolve the dissonance between self-perception and actions. People strive to maintain a positive view of themselves. If their behavior conflicts with this self-image, they may struggle to admit their actions. By framing their behavior as a response to external pressures, we allow them to recognize what they did without fully compromising their self-worth.

It's important to understand that empathy is not the same as agreement. Acknowledging someone's motivations doesn't mean endorsing their actions. In many of the criminal cases I've worked on—especially those involving child exploitation—I use this approach to foster communication. While I never agree with or excuse their behavior, I attempt to create an environment where they feel that, given their life experiences, I understand why some people make poor choices.

This distinction is crucial in sensitive conversations. Demonstrating understanding without approval can help the person feel less judged, opening the door for disclosure. By reframing actions as responses to external pressures rather than personal failings, we allow individuals to preserve their self-image while admitting to their behavior. Whether in an investigative interview or workplace conversation, this approach helps alleviate guilt and shame, making it easier for the person to open up. Empathy without agreement builds trust and fosters collaboration, turning defensiveness into dialogue.

A parent speaking with their child they believe is taking money from their purse or wallet says, "I understand taking things that don't belong to you is wrong, but when you're under stress, sometimes people make poor choices. Let's not compound the first mistake with another by denying what we both know to be the truth."

A business owner confronts an employee about internal theft: "Given the financial stress you were under, it's understandable that you might have seen this as your only option to support your family."

The approach in both examples acknowledges the difficult circumstances without condoning the other person's actions. It alleviates guilt, shows empathy, and reduces defensiveness, increasing the likelihood of an honest discussion.

(D)—Diminishing the Impact of the Person's Actions or Choices

By diminishing the seriousness or consequences, we can help mitigate the other person's fear of severe punishment or social judgment, making them more willing to confess. This technique reassures them that their actions are not as catastrophic as they might believe, which can be instrumental in obtaining a disclosure.

The fundamental psychological mechanism behind diminishing the other person's actions involves creating a perception in the person you are speaking to that their actions are understandable and less severe. This approach significantly impacts the suspect's mental state, reducing defensiveness and increasing their willingness to talk. When we tell someone, "It's not that big of a deal because everyone makes mistakes, and this is something that can be fixed," it normalizes the behavior, making the other person feel they are not alone in their wrongdoing.

Diminishing the impact of someone's actions effectively lowers a person's resistance to disclosure by making the consequences seem less dire. When the other person perceives the consequences of their actions as less severe, they are more likely to make a disclosure.

A loss prevention officer speaking with a young suspect accused of attempting to steal some clothes may say: "Look, this isn't the first time someone's been in this type of situation. It's not the end of the world. We have the items back, and they can be restocked. You made a poor choice. However, let's not compound that poor choice with another one by denying what another person saw you do, okay? What's important is that we sort this out and find a way to move forward."

A police officer investigating a case of a subject accused of spray-painting a wall might say: "It's not the end of the world. You're not the first person to make a mistake like this, and it's something we can take care of. Some elbow grease, dish soap, and a fresh coat of paint will look as good as new. Let's be up front about what happened so we can figure out how to make things right."

(D)—Developing a Personalized Narrative Using Stories, Metaphors, and Analogies

In addition to these techniques, using stories, analogies, and metaphors can make the suspect feel more comfortable and understood. These narrative tools can provide a framework for the suspect to relate to the interrogator's perspective, making the admission process less intimidating.

Storytelling

Stories can be powerful tools for humanizing communication and making the person you speak to feel less isolated. We can demonstrate empathy and understanding by sharing relevant stories and encouraging others to open up. For example, I often share a story about someone in a comparable situation who made a mistake but found a way to make amends. This can help the suspect see a path forward and feel less overwhelmed by their circumstances. Since the beginning of time, when our ancestors sat around the fire, they told stories. Stories captivate the imagination and cause people to listen. As I discussed, good barbecue and criminal interrogations are remarkably similar. The time spent preparing and conducting the interview is highly correlated with subsequent success. Too often, people don't get traction after a brief period and either give up or get emotional. Additionally, we can weave all of the "BUDDY" concepts into the narrative, making storytelling a highly effective strategy.

In storytelling, interviewing, and sales, relatability is crucial. People are more likely to engage with, remember, and be persuaded by content that resonates with their experiences and identities. This is why, when crafting stories, conducting criminal interviews, or making sales pitches, it's effective to draw parallels between the characters or scenarios presented and the individuals you are speaking with. The key is to make the characters or scenarios relatable to your audience. Think about the movies or books that captivate you—often, it's because you see a part of yourself in the characters or share something in common with the story's theme. This connection fosters a deeper emotional engagement, making the story more memorable and impactful.

For instance, if you are trying to teach a lesson or convey a message, framing it within a story where the protagonist shares similar struggles, goals, or values as your listener can make the story far more persuasive. A Stanford study on storytelling and memory retention reinforces this concept, revealing that students remembered 63% of the stories they were told but only 5% of the statistics they were presented with.[5] This finding emphasizes the power of storytelling in making information stick, especially when it resonates on a personal level.

In the context of criminal interviewing, storytelling can be a powerful tool for building rapport and breaking down resistance. When an interrogator tells a story that mirrors the suspect's life or situation, it can create a sense of empathy and understanding, making the suspect more willing to open up. As an interrogator, I frequently shared stories about people who made mistakes but found ways to make things right. If the story paralleled the suspect's circumstances, it would often lower the suspect's resistance level and cause them to be more inclined to confess.

The same principles apply to sales. A sales pitch is most effective when it feels like a story in which the customer is the hero. The pitch becomes more persuasive if the salesperson can paint a picture that aligns with the customer's life, showing how the product or service can solve their specific problems or enhance their lifestyle. People are more likely to make a purchase when they see themselves reflected in the story being told.

For instance, if selling a fitness product, a salesperson might tell a story about a customer who had similar fitness goals and achieved them with the help of the product. By making the story relatable, the salesperson taps into the customer's aspirations and desires, making the pitch more compelling.

Narrative Transportation

Narrative transportation refers to a psychological phenomenon where individuals become so deeply engaged in a story that they are "transported" into another world, temporarily losing awareness of their immediate surroundings and reality. This concept suggests that stories can profoundly impact an individual's beliefs, attitudes, and behaviors. When a person experiences narrative transportation, they are not just passively consuming a story; they are emotionally and cognitively immersed, feeling as though they are part of the narrative itself.

During this state, an individual's focus shifts entirely to the story, allowing them to forget their real-world concerns temporarily. The listener or reader might experience the characters' emotions as if they were their own. A well-told, rich story can also influence attitudes and beliefs, making the audience more likely to accept the narrative's premises and messages without critical scrutiny, leading to potential changes in their views and perceptions. The impact of a well-crafted story can be long-lasting, influencing the thoughts and feelings of the reader or viewer even after the narrative has ended.

Research on narrative transportation has shown that it can significantly influence an individual's beliefs and attitudes. A study found that participants deeply transported into a narrative were more likely to be persuaded by the story's messages. The study concluded that narrative transportation reduces counterarguing as the audience becomes more emotionally involved and less likely to evaluate the story's premises critically.[6] Some politicians are particularly adept at linking their proposed policies to compelling stories that resonate with their constituents, appealing to a broader audience.

Another study highlighted the importance of narrative transportation in marketing. The researchers found that stories that effectively transport consumers lead to higher levels of engagement and more favorable attitudes toward the brand. This effect was especially pronounced when the narrative was relatable and emotionally compelling.[7] For example, the day after the Super Bowl, people are often polled about the effectiveness of commercials, and those that tell a story tend to be the most well-received.

The Power of Analogies in Enhancing Communication and Disclosure

Analogies are a powerful tool in communication, especially in sensitive situations. They help simplify complex scenarios, making them more relatable and easier to understand. By comparing a person's situation to something familiar, we can reduce anxiety, foster empathy, and facilitate more open and honest dialogue. The scientific principles behind analogies reveal their effectiveness in enhancing communication and disclosure, rooted in cognitive psychology and neuroscience.

Analogies leverage the brain's natural ability to recognize patterns and draw connections between unrelated concepts. This cognitive process, known as analogical reasoning, involves mapping similarities between a familiar domain (the source) and a new or complex domain (the target).[8] This mapping process helps individuals understand abstract or emotionally charged situations by relating them to known experiences, making it easier for people to process and respond to information.

Analogies help break down complex situations into more manageable and relatable terms. My friend Kevin has successfully employed a particular analogy in hundreds of interviews, making it a staple in his approach.

"John, what brought us here today is in the rearview mirror. That represents the 'what'—the facts we already know. It's in the past, and we don't need to dwell on it. Instead, we need to focus on what's in front of us, which is the windshield. The windshield is much larger than the rearview mirror, symbolizing our future path. We should focus on understanding why you did what you did so we can move forward."

This analogy helps shift the suspect's mindset from the past to the present and future, encouraging them to open up about their motivations and intentions. By emphasizing the importance of looking ahead, Kevin effectively creates a more constructive and less confrontational environment, fostering better communication and increasing the likelihood of obtaining truthful information.

Normalizing the Situation

Analogies can also normalize a suspect's actions by comparing them to common mistakes. This approach reduces feelings of guilt and shame, making it easier for the suspect to discuss their behavior.

Analogies are particularly effective when tailored to an individual's background and interests. During a polygraph examination I was conducting on a law enforcement applicant, I discussed his background at length. When we got to leisure activities, I asked him what he liked to do in his free time. He said he liked to watch television. This answer wasn't telling, so I asked what he liked to watch. He said nature shows. This was better, but I wanted more specific details. I asked specifically what kind of nature shows he watched, and he mentioned a recent documentary about a hive of honeybees that he found interesting.

To find a deeper meaning, I asked what about the bee documentary he found fascinating. He said he was intrigued by how the bees coordinated their actions to protect the queen. I noted this but wasn't sure how it would help me later.

During the interaction, the applicant failed the polygraph regarding undisclosed information about serious crimes. When discussing this result, he revealed he had been a member of a street gang. He became apprehensive when talking about a violent incident involving an altercation with a rival gang. When I was discussing if he had used a firearm during this altercation, he appeared to show subtle nonverbal agreement. Drawing from his interest in honeybees, I used the following analogy:

Me: "Think about the rivalry between honeybees and killer bees. Killer bees migrate and take over territories without following rules, while honeybees protect their hive and queen. In your situation, were you a killer bee or a honeybee?"

Applicant (starts to cry): "I was a honeybee."

Me: "Were you just trying to protect what was important to you?"

Applicant: "Yes."

Me: "How many times did you 'sting' the rival gang member?"

Applicant: "Three."

It turned out he had shot a rival gang member several years before applying for a job in law enforcement. What began as an applicant interview turned into identifying a homicide suspect by focusing on his leisure activity and using tailored analogies.

Enhancing Empathy and Understanding

Analogies can also foster empathy by helping individuals see things from a different perspective. In another case, I interviewed a math teacher accused of child exploitation. I used his analytical background to frame the conversation.

"You're a very analytical person. Think of your life as an equation. Currently, the variables are all over the place, and things don't add up. Let's work together to balance this equation and find the truth." This analogy resonated with the math teacher, leading him to reflect on his actions and eventually admit to his involvement.

Building Rapport Through Tailored Analogies

Tailoring analogies to an individual's background and interests can significantly enhance rapport. For example, I once interviewed a suspect accused of homicide who had spent his entire adult life as a truck driver. He failed the polygraph examination concerning his alleged involvement in the crime. To understand the circumstances surrounding the crime, I employed an analogy based on his life as a truck driver.

"Consider the stringent regulations in your trucking life—driving hours, cargo limitations, speed restrictions. These rules keep you safe on the road. However, when you come home, it's a different story. Without those familiar rules and safeguards, you might feel out of control. This lack of control could lead someone to act out of character. Right now, we're stuck in a rut, spinning our tires. Let's put the chains on and get ourselves out of this situation."

This analogy helped the suspect relate his professional experiences to his personal life, leading to a confession.

(Y)—"Y" Is More Important Than "What"

The last part of the BUDDY framework emphasizes that the "why" behind someone's actions matters more than the "what" they did. In high-stakes conversations, it's easy to get caught up in *what* someone did—whether they made a mistake, told a lie, or broke your trust. But understanding *why* they acted that way is much more powerful. Unlocking the "why" often helps move the conversation toward truth and resolution. The *what* gives you the facts, but the *why* uncovers intent, motivation, and beliefs—key factors for building trust and creating meaningful connections.

When conducting interviews, I always focused on the "why." Asking someone *why* they did something opens the door to their story. When you understand their deeper motivations, you can steer the conversation, connect with them, and even use that insight to guide them toward a confession or solution.

This principle also works beyond investigative interviews. Leaders who only focus on results—the "what"—might frustrate their team members by ignoring the reasons behind their actions. For instance, if an employee misses a deadline, a typical response might be reprimanding them for not finishing on time. But if you ask *why* they missed it, you might discover they were overwhelmed or didn't get precise instructions. With this insight, you can solve the root issue, prevent future mistakes, and build trust with the employee.

Focusing on the "why" can help avoid unnecessary arguments in personal relationships. Let's say a friend cancels plans they had with you at the last minute. You might feel hurt or annoyed if you only look at the what. But if you ask *why*, you might learn they've been going through a tough time or just needed some time to themselves. That shift from frustration to understanding can turn what could have been a fight into an opportunity for a deeper connection.

Sales professionals and negotiators can also benefit from focusing on the "why." If a client hesitates to make a purchase, focusing on *what* they say—like concerns about price—might mean missing the chance to address the real issue. If you ask *why* the price bothers them, you might learn they're worried the product won't meet their needs. By addressing that fear directly, rather than sticking to the numbers, you open the door to an agreement.

Prioritizing the "why" gives you insight. When people feel understood, they're more likely to trust you, open up, and work with you. The *what* tells you what happened, but the *why* reveals the true drivers of behavior—intent, beliefs, and motivation.

Mastering the art of finding the "why" takes curiosity, patience, and avoiding jumping to conclusions. Instead of reacting to someone's actions right away, step back and dig deeper. Whether in interviews, business, or personal life, the most meaningful connections—and the best outcomes—come from understanding the "why" behind the actions.

I once assisted a police department on a robbery case at a local convenience store. They suspected one of the employees had helped plan the crime with his friends. I conducted a polygraph on the main suspect, and he failed.

Me: "John, it's clear you were involved in helping a couple of people take the money from the store."

Suspect: "What?"

Me: "We're not here to debate whether you did it. We've got security footage, cell phone records, text messages, and your failed polygraph proving your involvement in the situation. That's the *what*. I don't want to focus on that. I want to understand *why* you felt the need to do it. People make mistakes, and if we can understand the situation, we can put things in context. Most importantly, no one was hurt, and the money can be returned. Many folks would understand if this happened because you were struggling with bills, and someone gave you a bad idea."

Suspect (leaning forward/confession posture): "Times have been tough lately."

Me: "I get that. Stress can push people to make bad decisions. Is that what happened here? Were you having financial trouble, and someone gave you a bad idea?"

Suspect: "I just don't want to get anyone else in trouble."

Me: "I respect that—you're trying to take responsibility. But I don't want you taking the full hit for someone else's bad idea. Let's stay focused on the *why*. If you did this because you were in a tough spot and someone took advantage of that, let's talk about it and move forward. So, whose idea was it?"

Suspect: "My buddy came to me last week. He said we could help each other out."

By focusing on *why* John acted the way he did, I uncovered his real motive—financial pressure. This understanding allowed me to build rapport with him and guide the conversation toward a confession and resolution.

Now that we have laid out the application of the BUDDY technique, let's discuss how we can see if we are making progress in resolving the issue.

STEP 4: I—IDENTIFY SIGNS OF RECEPTIVITY

Objections

At this point in the conversation, the other person may object—a natural and often encouraging sign that you're getting closer to a resolution. Unlike a denial, which shuts down dialogue entirely, an objection indicates that the individual is not outright rejecting your assertions but rather expressing hesitation or discomfort.

This hesitation offers an opportunity: They're not saying "no"—they're saying "not yet."

In sales, negotiations, and interrogations, objections serve a similar role: They reveal underlying concerns, doubts, or excuses that the subject offers to resist the desired outcome—whether it's making a purchase, agreeing to terms, or confessing to involvement in a crime. Objections signal that the person engages with the conversation and weighs the possibility, even if they're not ready to commit.

In sales and interrogations, an objection isn't the end of the road—it's a turning point. The subject's resistance suggests they're open to further discussion but need help resolving internal conflicts or uncertainties. A skilled communicator will acknowledge the objection without dismissing it, using it as a chance to guide the conversation forward.

To deal with an objection, I developed an acronym called ART. This approach involves three steps:

1. **Accept the Objection**
   In both sales and interrogations, acknowledging the objection shows that you are listening and respecting the other person's perspective. This builds rapport and makes the other person feel understood, which can lower their defenses.

2. **Repackage**
   Use the objection to further the conversation to align with your goal. For example, acknowledging budget concerns in sales can lead to discussing cost-saving benefits. In interrogations, acknowledging a suspect's character can lead to discussing how the situation might have unfolded differently than intended.

3. **Turn It Around**
   Redirect the conversation to align with your desired outcome. In sales, this might mean reframing a budget objection into a discussion about long-term value. In interrogations, it might mean shifting the focus from denying intent to explaining the circumstances that led to the incident.

When you are involved in a discussion that involves a difference of opinion, it is effective to agree with part of the other person's argument before pivoting to make your point. Acknowledging the other person's position often builds rapport and makes you appear reasonable before gently turning the conversation toward your desired outcome. By validating your counterpart's feelings or beliefs, you disarm them and make them more open to your argument. This can also prevent the conversation from turning confrontational and instead shift it toward finding common ground. Here are some examples of ART in action.

Criminal Interview Example
Objection: "I would never intentionally hurt anyone!"

- **Accept:** "I agree with you."
- **Repackage:** "That makes complete sense; you don't seem like someone who wakes up in the morning with bad intentions and looks to hurt another person."
- **Turn It Around:** "Sometimes, situations spiral out of control, and things happen that we never intended. Let's talk about how things escalated so we can clearly understand what happened."

Sales Example:
Objection: "I need to think about it."

- **Accept:** "I totally understand that you want to make the right decision."
- **Repackage:** "It's important to weigh your options, and it's clear you're considering what's best for you."
- **Turn It Around:** "Let's walk through any questions or concerns you have now so you have all the information you need to feel confident about your choice."

Now, after understanding how to deal with objections effectively, let's look at other verbal and nonverbal signs that show we are moving toward resolution.

- **Forward Leaning:** The suspect starts to lean slightly forward, resting their elbows on their knees. This shift suggests they are becoming more engaged in conversation and less concerned with maintaining a defensive barrier.
- **Slumped Shoulders:** The suspect's shoulders droop, indicating they are releasing some tension. This physical change shows that they might be feeling the weight of the situation and are moving toward a state of emotional vulnerability.
- **Downward Gaze:** The suspect avoids direct eye contact, looking down at the floor or their hands. This behavior can signify contemplation and an internal struggle with their potential decision to make a disclosure. It suggests that they are feeling guilt or shame about their actions.
- **Elevated Sighs:** The suspect lets out a deep sigh, a clear sign of emotional release. This sound can indicate that they are mentally preparing to disclose information they have been withholding.

Another effective technique to reengage someone and encourage them to move toward a potential confession is to ask them to read or look at something related to the situation that you have in your possession. This action requires the suspect to physically lean forward, which can effectively reset their emotional state, akin to pressing "control-alt-delete" on a computer. By breaking the negative body language and emotional state they may be anchored in, this physical shift can help them move away from a defensive posture. Consequently, they are less likely to revert to entirely negative body language and might remain in a more neutral or even open state.

At this point, we must realize that we must move on to the next stage. In doing so, we may move closer, soften our tone of voice, and lower our volume. We may also utilize touch strategically to connect with the other subject. Now, it is time to move on to the last step.

STEP 5: T—TRANSITION TO ADMISSION OR AGREEMENT

At this point in the conversation, we've built rapport, identified deception, and carefully guided the person to a place where telling the truth feels like a relief—not a risk. Now, we're aiming for admission or agreement. However, we don't want to appear desperate or pushy.

One technique I often use here is called the bad/good option. It's a psychological approach used in many investigative interviewing frameworks when the person seems close to making an admission. Ideally, you would present two versions of the same event—one that casts the person in a more negative light (the bad option) and another that allows them to save face (the good option). You're providing them a choice while leading them toward the option that's easier to admit and still consistent with their identity.[9]

Think of it like this: Most people prefer to be seen as someone who made a mistake rather than as someone who's evil. So, you give them that path. Here's an example from a homicide case I worked on in St. Louis.

Me: "You didn't wake up at 8 AM this morning with ill will in your heart, looking to hurt someone, did you?"

Suspect: "Nah."

Me: "You just got wrapped up in a crazy set of circumstances and made a mistake?"

Suspect: "Yeah."

Another hypothetical scenario involves a parent whose child is upset because their favorite toy is missing, and you know one of the other children took it. Instead of accusing, you create a soft landing for the truth.

Parent: "You didn't take your sister's toy just to be mean and upset her, did you?"

Child: "No . . ."

Parent: "You just really liked it, and didn't think it would be a big deal?"

Child: "Yeah . . ."

The Power of the Presumptive Question and "What Else?"

Continuing along the good/bad option strategy, presumptive questions are one of the most effective ways to guide a conversation toward truth and meaningful disclosure. These questions operate on the assumption that the behavior or event in question has already occurred. Rather than asking if something happened, a presumptive question implies that it did—and invites the other person to clarify or explain. This subtle shift lowers defenses, makes outright denial less likely, and moves the person from a guarded yes-or-no mindset into a more relaxed storytelling mode.

The Follow-Up That Opens the Floodgates: "What Else?"

Once someone makes an initial admission, following up with a simple, calm "What else?" can be one of the most powerful tools in your conversational arsenal. It's open-ended and nonthreatening, and it signals that you're paying attention, that you expect more, and that it's okay to continue. It implies that more information exists—and often, it does. Most people reveal sensitive information in stages. That first admission is usually just a way of testing the waters to see how you will respond. Asking "What else?" permits them to go further. It helps them transition from dipping a toe into the truth to diving all the way in. I have found that the actual substance of a disclosure rarely comes until I've heard the person say, "That's it," or "There's nothing else." Contrast this with a question like "Is there anything else we need to talk about?"—which subtly suggests there might not be. That phrasing places the subject in control of the exit ramp. It makes it easier for them to withhold information and convince themselves that what has been shared is enough. A slight shift—from "Is there anything else?" to "What else?"—puts the momentum back in your hands and, more importantly, keeps the door to truth wide open.

Case Study: Parent and Child

Imagine a parent hears the unmistakable rustle of chip bags just before dinner. Then the pantry door opens again . . . and again. Instead of confronting or accusing, the parent leans on the power of the presumptive question.

Parent: "Hey, Sydney, when you grabbed those chips before dinner, was it because you were really hungry or just kind of bored?"

Child: "I was hungry."

Parent: "I understand. What else did you eat?"

Child: "Cookies."

Parent: "Okay. What else?"

Child: "That was it."

This strategy works because it removes the fear of punishment and replaces it with an opportunity for ownership. This same approach works in interrogation rooms, classrooms, boardrooms, and kitchen tables. Whether you're a parent, investigator, or teacher, your goal is the same: to create an environment where truth feels safer than silence. Presumptive questions help uncover the truth—and "What else?" helps you get all of it.

Now that we have examined the steps to getting someone to make an admission after they have been deceptive, let us combine the tactics into a complete package that you can employ during your daily interactions.

CONCLUSION

Connection to Confession Blueprint

"The beautiful thing about learning is that
nobody can take it away from you."
—B.B. King

As we bring this journey through the art and science of communication to a close, it's essential to reflect on the principles explored throughout the book. Drawing on my career with the United States Secret Service, the lessons here offer practical tools to enhance your communication skills in personal relationships, business settings, or high-stakes situations. These insights transcend law enforcement, applying to any interaction, from a critical negotiation to a conversation over coffee.

Communication is the foundation for personal and professional success—empowering you to connect meaningfully, earn trust, and foster cooperation. Mastering communication isn't about manipulation; it's about creating an environment where others feel safe, valued, and heard—an atmosphere that encourages people to open up. I've learned that people rarely share their truths without feeling comfortable. They protect what matters to them and guard their vulnerabilities. Your task isn't to extract information forcefully—it's to create trust through empathy, timing, and precision, making it easier for others to choose truth over deception.

My time conducting interviews and polygraphs showed me that confession isn't always about guilt—it's often a release, an unburdening. People often need a patient listener who won't interrupt, judge, or manipulate.

Throughout this book, we explored tools that demonstrate that communication is more than words. Detecting deception, building trust, and fostering connection require intentional effort—a focus on how you present yourself, listen, and engage with the person across from you. The following steps can enhance your communication skills and foster more meaningful connections with others.

STEP 1: PREPARE

Preparation is the bedrock of successful communication. It goes beyond simply knowing what you plan to say—it's about developing a deep understanding of the other person's background, motivations, concerns, and likely responses. This thorough preparation becomes even more critical in high-stakes situations, where every word and action can influence outcomes. However, the same principle applies to any meaningful conversation, whether you are negotiating a business deal, resolving conflict in a personal relationship, or preparing for an important professional discussion.

When you take the time to "do your homework," you gain the knowledge and insight to navigate complex interactions confidently. It helps you engage more effectively, reducing anxiety and building trust by showing the other person that you have invested time and care into the interaction.

Preparation isn't just about being ready for what you expect but equipping yourself to handle the unexpected. By fully committing to this foundational step, you can confidently approach each conversation, fostering deeper connections, defusing potential tension, and guiding interactions toward successful outcomes. Whether the stakes are personal or professional, preparation empowers you to engage thoughtfully, making every conversation a step toward greater understanding and stronger relationships.

STEP 2: MANAGE YOUR ANXIETY AND BUILD CONFIDENCE

Here are practical strategies to calm your nerves and enhance your confidence prior to the interaction.

- **Breathing Exercises:** Practice box breathing before an interaction to reduce anxiety.
- **Walk-Through Exercises:** Strategically plan and rehearse for the specific interaction.
- **Imitating Top Performers:** Learn by emulating successful individuals in your initial stages.
- **Maintaining Physical Fitness:** Maintain physical fitness to reduce stress and improve overall well-being.

STEP 3: MASTER YOUR FIRST IMPRESSION AND IMPACT BY USING ALL FIVE SENSES

We have explored how to leverage all five senses to enhance the impact of our communication, particularly in making first impressions.

- **Professional Appearance:** Your clothes can shape others' perceptions of your authority and confidence.
- **The Eyebrow Flash:** A quick raising of the eyebrows at introduction as a friend signal.
- **The Importance of a Subtle Smile:** Conveys warmth, approachability, and confidence.

- **Forward Lean:** Indicates interest and engagement.
- **Open Posture / Ventral Fronting:** Signals openness and honesty.
- **Head Nods:** Indicates understanding and agreement.
- **Varying Vocal Pitch and Tone:** Enhances interest in your message and reduces perception of stress.
- **Lowering Volume at Sensitive Moments:** Creates a sense of artificial privacy.
- **The Power of Silence:** Increases the impact of your message. Silence creates space for reflection and often reveals more than words ever could. It takes patience to resist the urge to fill every pause, but those who master this art will discover that silence invites truth. The best communicators are not those who dominate conversations but those who create the space for others to share their truths.
- **Importance of Vocal Warm-Ups:** Ensures your voice is more expressive and articulate.
- **The World's Best Handshake:** A warm, dry handshake that matches the other person's firmness is essential in making a positive first impression.

STEP 4: CHOOSE THE RIGHT TIME AND PLACE

One of the most valuable lessons I have learned is timing—what the Greeks call *kairos*, the art of seizing the perfect moment. Knowing when to speak and remain silent can mean the difference between building trust and encountering resistance. Communication is not just about what you say—it's about how, when, and where you say it. A poorly timed comment can derail a conversation, while a well-placed pause can unlock unexpected insights.

Equally crucial is presence—the ability to show up fully, both physically and emotionally. Presence goes beyond words; it is conveyed through body language, facial expressions, and how you engage with others. When people feel discomfort, they tend to withdraw. However, leaning into those moments—through subtle actions like a forward lean, a nod, or soft eye contact—signals attentiveness, empathy, and care. These small gestures are often the foundation of trust, quietly communicating *I see you. I hear you. I value you.*

Another critical element is privacy. People don't share their secrets in public—they confide in private. Creating the right environment for meaningful conversation requires attention to these subtle details. For example, planning a discussion after lunch can ensure that hunger or fatigue don't interfere with focus or decision-making. Mastering these nuances—timing, presence, and privacy—sets the stage for authentic connections where trust can flourish.

STEP 5: USING ETHICAL INFLUENCE IN COMMUNICATION TO SCORE TRUST

Applying the SCORE framework lets you authentically connect, ethically influence, and build meaningful relationships. Active listening is crucial once an emotional balance is established.

- **Social Proof.** People often follow the actions and beliefs of the majority, especially in uncertain situations. Showing that others have already taken a specific action or adopted a perspective provides validation and encourages others to do the same.
- **Curiosity.** Genuine curiosity is a powerful tool for fostering engagement. When you demonstrate interest in others by asking thoughtful questions and listening actively, they are more likely to share information and form a connection.
- **Observation.** Effective communicators pay attention to more than just words; they also notice nonverbal cues, body language, and emotional shifts. Observing these subtle signals enables you

to adjust your approach in real time, enhancing understanding and responsiveness.

- **Respect.** Trust and cooperation are founded on respect. Even in disagreements, treating others with dignity creates an environment where they feel safe to express themselves. Respect strengthens relationships and increases the likelihood of honest and open dialogue.
- **Exchange.** The principle of reciprocity drives human interactions. When you provide value—whether through favors, insights, or generosity—you create a natural psychological pull for others to reciprocate, thereby strengthening connections and fostering goodwill.

By incorporating these five elements into your communication strategy, you become a more persuasive, empathetic, and effective communicator. Whether in leadership, negotiation, sales, or personal relationships, applying the SCORE framework allows you to navigate conversations with confidence and achieve more positive and lasting outcomes.

STEP 6: UTILIZE ACTIVE LISTENING AND MIMICRY

I emphasize the importance of active listening using the SEEMS framework:

- **S**—Summarizing the conversation to ensure clarity.
- **E**—Empathic statements to acknowledge emotions.
- **E**—Emotion labeling to identify feelings aloud.
- **M**—Minimal encouragers, such as nods or brief affirmations, to invite more sharing.
- **S**—Signals of interest, like sustained eye contact, to convey engagement.

Mimicry is an essential, often subconscious, tool in human interaction. It is the natural tendency to reflect another person's body language, speech patterns, or gestures, which helps establish rapport and increase feelings of connection. Research shows that when someone subtly mirrors another person's movements or tone, it activates a sense of trust and familiarity, making interactions smoother and more persuasive.

When combined with active listening, mimicry strengthens relationships by fostering a sense of unity. Whether in negotiations, interviews, or personal conversations, mirroring helps individuals feel understood, making them more likely to open up and engage honestly. However, the most important takeaway is that listening is an act of respect. When you give someone your full attention—without interrupting or imposing your views—you send a powerful message: *You matter.*

STEP 7: DETECT AND ADDRESS DECEPTION

Detecting deception is a crucial skill in high-stakes communication. When someone deceives you, they typically engage in one or more of the following actions within seconds of being asked a yes or no question, as outlined in the acronym DECEIVES:

- **D**—Delay.
- **E**—Exclusive qualifiers.
- **C**—Confronting the questioner.
- **E**—Emotionally inconsistent.
- **I**—Inserting truthful information into a lie.
- **V**—Verbal/nonverbal disconnect.
- **E**—Evasion.
- **S**—Shifting vocal inflection.

Remember, always ask yourself, "Did they answer the question?"

STEP 8: BE THEIR BUDDY TO OBTAIN INFORMATION

Once you've identified deception, the next step isn't confrontation—it's connection. The BUDDY approach is used at this critical moment to lower defenses, create psychological safety, and guide someone toward telling the truth. It's a compassionate and strategic way to transition from resistance to revelation.

- B—Blaming something or someone else for the person's actions.
- U—Understanding of reasoning behind the person's actions.
- D—Diminishing the impact of the person's actions or choices.
- D—Developing a personalized narrative using stories and analogies.
- Y—"Y" is more important than "what."

As we reach the end of this journey, remember: every conversation is an opportunity—to learn, to connect, and to build trust. Communication isn't a onetime achievement; it's a lifelong skill that sharpens through practice, reflection, and intentional growth.

This idea was vividly demonstrated in the first Ultimate Fighting Championship (UFC) in 1993. Fighters from different disciplines—boxing, kickboxing, karate, Brazilian Jiu-Jitsu—each believed their fighting method was the best. But it was Royce Gracie, a calm BJJ practitioner, who stunned the world by dominating opponents far larger and stronger. His success didn't just win a title—it changed how fighters trained forever.

Yet within a few short years, the landscape evolved. Early specialists in Brazilian Jiu-Jitsu, who initially dominated by relying solely on ground fighting, soon faced defeat at the hands of more well-rounded fighters—those who combined striking, wrestling, and submission skills. The first UFC proved a point, but it also sparked an arms race of adaptation.

Fighters who remained beholden to a single style quickly found themselves left behind.

The lesson? Mastery comes not from rigid loyalty to one approach, but from blending, adapting, and evolving. This principle also applies to communication. Exceptional communicators don't depend on a single trick or technique. They observe, listen, and adapt. Genuine connection isn't about exerting control—it's about being present. This means being fully engaged and authentically human, and being open to understanding what others may find difficult to express.

Ask the better question—the one that cuts beneath the surface. Notice what others miss—the pause, the glance, the story hidden between the words. Create the space where truth feels safe enough to emerge. Because the truth rarely arrives on command. It waits. It watches. It tests whether you are worthy to receive it.

So be patient. Be present. And when the moment finally comes—whether in an interrogation room, a boardroom, or your own living room—look the other person in the eye, lean in just enough, and invite them to do the one thing that matters most: *Tell you everything.*

ACKNOWLEDGMENTS

This book is the culmination of years of experience, learning, and collaboration. It would not have been possible without the unwavering support of so many remarkable individuals who have shaped my journey and enriched my life.

To my wife, Stephanie—you have been my rock and source of strength throughout my Secret Service career. Your love, patience, and belief in me provided the foundation I needed to navigate even the most demanding moments. Despite enduring 17 missed anniversaries and countless sacrifices, your steadfast dedication never wavered.

This book holds even deeper significance because it was written during your courageous and successful battle with cancer. Even as you endured chemotherapy, you found the resolve to edit early drafts—using it as a momentary escape from the weight of treatment. Your resilience, determination, and partnership inspire me more than words can express. You are my confidante, my greatest source of encouragement, and the reason this book exists.

To my children, Andrew and Sydney—you are my greatest joy and motivation. Your curiosity, energy, and boundless enthusiasm push me daily to be a better father, husband, and professional. You are my proudest achievements and the brightest lights in my life.

To my parents, Ron and Mary Beeler—your commitment to public service and teaching instilled in me the values that have guided my life and career. Your selflessness and constant encouragement provided the foundation for everything I've accomplished. You taught me resilience, integrity, and the importance of giving back—lessons that have shaped my life. You both sacrificed so much to make sure your children were put in a position to succeed in life.

To my sisters, Beth, Ronda, and Lynn—thank you for your patience, support, and laughter over the years. Those shared moments around the dinner table deepened our bond, sharpened my ability to tell stories, and reinforced the power of humor in facing life's challenges.

To my former Secret Service colleagues—I am profoundly grateful for your camaraderie, professionalism, and unwavering dedication to our mission. A special thank you to Lee Swafford, Desmond O'Neill, Ryan Shiplett, Bryan Perry, and Jim McGettigan—your mentorship and the countless hours we spent in interview rooms across the country form the very foundation of this book.

To my first partner at the Secret Service, John "Tino" McCabe—thank you for keeping me safe and teaching me the ropes on the streets of Chicago. As a third-generation Chicago police officer, your experience and guidance were invaluable. You've forgotten more about policing than most cops will learn in a career.

To my mentor, Brian Leary—you are the most gifted polygraph examiner and interrogator I have ever had the privilege of learning from. Your unmatched ability to connect with people and your guidance throughout my career have left an enduring mark. The lessons you imparted echo through every principle shared in this book.

To Chris Hadnagy, Dr. Abbie Maroño, Robin Dreeke, Dr. Paul Zak, An Gaiser, Scott Klein, Brendan Hickey, Blair Brown, Jean Beeler, Jesse Zbinden-Brassard, Dave Escobales, Tobias Hyman, Raluca Stewart, Beth Kincaid, Mary Beeler, and Ryan Fretts—thank you for your invaluable insights and expertise during the editing process. Your feedback helped elevate this book and clarify its vision, and I am deeply grateful for your guidance.

To Dr. Stacy Cecchet—thank you for helping me and many of my colleagues navigate the emotional weight of the horrific stories we encountered in law enforcement, especially those in child exploitation.

Your guidance has been instrumental in dealing with the darkest aspects of our work.

To Matt Holt and the extraordinary team at BenBella Books—thank you for believing in this first-time author and helping turn my ideas into a cohesive, impactful work. A special thanks to Katie Dickman, whose meticulous attention to detail and tireless effort transformed countless drafts into the polished final product you hold today.

To my students—you are a continual source of inspiration and growth. Your curiosity, enthusiasm, and willingness to learn remind me of the importance of being "the most interested man in the room." You push me to dig deeper, refine my craft, and strive for excellence every day.

Finally, to the reader—thank you for taking this journey with me. Whether you are in law enforcement, business, or personal development, I hope this book equips you with the tools to master communication, resolve conflicts, and build meaningful connections.

NOTES

CHAPTER 1

1. Janine Willis and Alexander Todorov, "First Impressions: Making Up Your Mind After a 100-Ms Exposure to a Face," *Psychological Science* 17, no. 7 (2006): 592–98.
2. Raymond S. Nickerson, "Confirmation Bias: A Ubiquitous Phenomenon in Many Guises," *Review of General Psychology* 2, no. 2 (1998): 175–220.
3. Aldert Vrij, "Why Professionals Fail to Catch Liars and How They Can Improve," *Legal and Criminological Psychology* 9, no. 2 (2004): 159–81.

CHAPTER 2

1. Harvard University, Carnegie Foundation, and Stanford Research Center, "Greatest Factor in Job Success: Soft Skills," eDynamic Learning, 2023. Accessed March 4, 2025, https://www.edynamiclearning.com/greatest-factor-in-job-success-soft-skills/.
2. Klaus R. Scherer, "Vocal Markers of Emotion: Comparing Induction and Acting," *Journal of Nonverbal Behavior* 37, no. 2 (2013): 95–115.
3. Stephen E. Lucas, *The Art of Public Speaking*, 12th ed. (New York: McGraw-Hill Education, 2015), chapter 2.
4. Valerie Manusov and Miles L. Patterson, *The SAGE Handbook of Nonverbal Communication* (Thousand Oaks, CA: SAGE Publications, 2006).
5. Theodore H. White, *The Making of the President 1960* (New York: Harper Perennial, 2010).

CHAPTER 4

1. Hajo Adam and Adam D. Galinsky, "Enclothed Cognition," *Journal of Experimental Social Psychology* 48, no. 4 (2012): 918–25.
2. Joseph Petrilli, Laura Jones, and Marissa Vulikh, "The Impact of Professional Dress on Performance in a Remote Work Environment," *Journal of Applied Psychology* 106, no. 8 (2021): 1114–24.
3. Sarah Kleinman, "Maintaining Professionalism in a Hybrid Work Environment," *Journal of Corporate Culture* 14, no. 1 (2022): 45–58.
4. Joe Navarro and Marvin Karlins, *What Every Body Is Saying: An Ex-FBI Agent's Guide to Speed-Reading People* (New York: HarperCollins, 2008).
5. Chris L. Kleinke, "Gaze and Eye Contact: A Research Review," *Psychological Bulletin* 100, no. 1 (1986): 78–100.
6. Ann L. Drolet and Michael W. Morris, "Rapport in Conflict Resolution: Accounting for How Face-to-Face Contact Fosters Mutual Cooperation in Mixed-Motive Conflicts," *Journal of Experimental Social Psychology* 36, no. 1 (2000): 26–50.
7. David Matsumoto, Mark G. Frank, and Hyi Sung Hwang, *Nonverbal Communication: Science and Applications* (Thousand Oaks, CA: Sage Publications, 2012).
8. Lee A. Harker and Dacher Keltner, "Expressions of Positive Emotion in Women's College Yearbook Pictures and Their Relationship to Personality and Life Outcomes Across Adulthood," *Journal of Personality and Social Psychology* 80, no. 1 (2001): 112–24.
9. Tina L. Kraft and Sarah D. Pressman, "Grin and Bear It: The Influence of Manipulated Facial Expression on the Stress Response," *Psychological Science* 23, no. 11 (2012): 1372–78.
10. Leon VandeCreek and T. Jackson, "The Influence of Active Listening and Nonverbal Communication on Perception of Others," *Journal of Counseling Psychology* 41, no. 2 (1994): 246–52.
11. Albert Mehrabian, *Nonverbal Communication* (New Brunswick, NJ: Aldine Transaction, 1972).
12. Judee K. Burgoon, Laura K. Guerrero, and Kory Floyd, *Nonverbal Communication* (New York: Routledge, 2016).
13. Allan Pease and Barbara Pease, *The Definitive Book of Body Language* (New York: Bantam, 2004).

14. Paul Ekman, "Basic Emotions," in *Handbook of Cognition and Emotion*, eds. T. Dalgleish and M. J. Power (Chichester, UK: John Wiley & Sons, 1999), 45–60.
15. Fritz Strack, Leonard L. Martin, and Sabine Stepper, "Inhibiting and Facilitating Conditions of the Human Smile: A Nonobtrusive Test of the Facial Feedback Hypothesis," *Journal of Personality and Social Psychology* 54, no. 5 (1988): 768–77.
16. Paul Ekman, *Telling Lies: Clues to Deceit in the Marketplace, Politics, and Marriage* (New York: W.W. Norton & Company, 1992).

CHAPTER 5

1. William Apple, Lee A. Streeter, and Robert M. Krauss, "Effects of Pitch and Speech Rate on Personal Attributions," *Journal of Personality and Social Psychology* 37, no. 5 (1979): 715–27.
2. James Brunner and Lisa Stock, "Speaking Rate as a Measure of Stress," *Psychological Reports* 100, no. 1 (2007): 74–84.
3. Beverly L. Brown, Howard Giles, and John N. Thakerar, "Speaker Evaluations as a Function of Speech Rate, Accent, and Context," *Language & Communication* 5, no. 3 (1985): 207–20.
4. Owen Hargie, *Skilled Interpersonal Communication: Research, Theory and Practice*, 5th ed. (New York: Routledge, 2011).
5. Marielle Stel and Ad van Knippenberg, "The Role of Facial Mimicry in the Recognition of Affect," *Psychological Science* 19, no. 10 (2008): 984–85.
6. Chris Voss, *Never Split the Difference: Negotiating as If Your Life Depended on It* (New York: Harper Business, 2016).
7. Annett Schirmer and Sonja A. Kotz, "Beyond the Right Hemisphere: Brain Mechanisms Mediating Vocal Emotional Processing," *Trends in Cognitive Sciences* 10, no. 1 (2006): 24–30.
8. Karol Jean Tusing and James Price Dillard, "The Sounds of Dominance: Vocal Precursors of Dominance During Interpersonal Influence," *Human Communication Research* 26, no. 1 (2000): 148–71.
9. Wendy Levinson et al., "Physician-Patient Communication: The Relationship with Malpractice Claims Among Primary Care Physicians and Surgeons," *JAMA* 277, no. 7 (1997): 553–59.
10. "Thatcher's Voice: A Shrill, Bossy Woman," *The Guardian*, April 20, 1980.

11. Tim Bale, *The Iron Lady: The Definitive Biography of Margaret Thatcher* (New York: Doubleday, 2008).
12. John Carreyrou, *Bad Blood: Secrets and Lies in a Silicon Valley Startup* (New York: Knopf, 2018).
13. Marc D. Pell and Anuja Jaywant, "How Stressful Are Those Voices? Stress-Related Changes in Pitch and Speech Rate as a Function of Stressor Type," *Applied Psycholinguistics* 25, no. 3 (2004): 373–93.
14. Merrill Hiscock and Marcel Kinsbourne, "Attention and the Right-Ear Advantage: What Is the Connection?" *Brain and Cognition* 76, no. 2 (2011): 263–75.
15. Robert T. Sataloff, *Professional Voice: The Science and Art of Clinical Care*, 3rd ed. (San Diego: Plural Publishing, 2005).
16. Herbert H. Clark and Jean E. Fox Tree, "Using Uh and Um in Spontaneous Speaking," *Cognition* 84, no. 1 (2002): 73–111.
17. Margaret L. McLaughlin and Michael J. Cody, "Awkward Silences: Behavioral Antecedents and Consequences of the Conversational Lapse," *Human Communication Research* 8, no. 4 (1982): 299–316.
18. Howard Waitzkin, "Doctor-Patient Communication: Clinical Implications of Social Scientific Research," *JAMA* 252, no. 17 (1984): 2441–46.

CHAPTER 6

1. William Schneider, *Vocal Mastery: Techniques for Professional Voice Care* (New York: Voice Health Press, 2017).
2. Jane Williams, *Body Language Secrets: The Science of Handshakes and Other Professional Gestures* (San Francisco: Gesture Press, 2018).
3. Sanda Dolcos and Florin Dolcos, "The Power of a Handshake: Neural Correlates of Evaluative Judgments in Observed Social Interactions," *Journal of Cognitive Neuroscience* 24, no. 12 (2012): 2292–2305.

CHAPTER 7

1. Hendrik Schifferstein, "Effects of Ambient Scent on Gambling Behavior," *Journal of Behavioral Addictions* 5, no. 2 (2006): 142–49.

2. Kendall J. Eskine, Natalie A. Kacinik, and Jesse J. Prinz, "A Bad Taste in the Mouth: Gustatory Disgust Influences Moral Judgment," *Psychological Science* 22, no. 3 (2011): 295–99.
3. William J. Havlena and Morris B. Holbrook, "The Varieties of Consumption Experience: Comparing Two Typologies of Emotion in Consumer Behavior," *Journal of Consumer Research* 13, no. 3 (1986): 394–404.
4. Rachel S. Herz, "A Naturalistic Analysis of Autobiographical Memories Triggered by Olfactory Visual and Auditory Stimuli," *Chemical Senses* 29, no. 3 (2004): 217–24.
5. Robert A. Baron, "The Sweet Smell of . . . Helping: Effects of Pleasant Ambient Fragrance on Prosocial Behavior in Shopping Malls," *Personality and Social Psychology Bulletin* 23, no. 5 (1997): 498–503.
6. Panagiota Kritsidima, Tim Newton, and Koula Asimakopoulou, "The Effects of Lavender Scent on Dental Patient Anxiety Levels: A Cluster Randomized-Controlled Trial," *Community Dentistry and Oral Epidemiology* 38, no. 1 (2010): 83–87.
7. Miguel A. Diego, Tiffany Jones, and Nancy A. Field, "Aromatherapy Positively Affects Mood, EEG Patterns of Alertness and Math Computations," *International Journal of Neuroscience* 96, no. 3–4 (1998): 217–24.
8. Johann Lehrner et al., "Ambient Odors of Orange and Lavender Reduce Anxiety and Improve Mood in a Dental Office," *Physiology & Behavior* 86, no. 1–2 (2005): 92–95.
9. Rika Sakamoto et al., "Effectiveness of Aromatherapy in Reducing Anxiety and Stress in Preoperative Patients," *Psychiatry and Clinical Neurosciences* 59, no. 4 (2005): 393–98.
10. Mark Moss et al., "Aromas of Rosemary and Peppermint Essential Oils Enhance Memory and Cognition in Healthy Adults," *International Journal of Neuroscience* 116, no. 10 (2006): 1519–32.
11. Morton Deutsch, "A Theory of Cooperation and Competition," *Human Relations* 2, no. 2 (1949): 129–52.
12. Richard Wrangham, *Catching Fire: How Cooking Made Us Human* (New York: Basic Books, 2009).
13. Robin I. M. Dunbar, "Breaking Bread: The Functions of Social Eating," *Adaptive Human Behavior and Physiology* 3, no. 3 (2017): 198–211.

14. Kevin M. Kniffin et al., "Eating Together at the Firehouse: How Workplace Commensality Relates to the Performance of Firefighters," *Human Performance* 28, no. 4 (2015): 281–306.
15. Charles Spence, Maria Mancini, and Gijs Huisman, "Digital Commensality: Eating and Drinking in the Company of Technology," *Frontiers in Psychology* 10 (2019): 2252.
16. Stephen W. Porges, *The Polyvagal Theory: Neurophysiological Foundations of Emotions, Attachment, Communication, and Self-Regulation* (New York: W.W. Norton & Company, 2011).
17. Erica J. Boothby, Margaret S. Clark, and John A. Bargh, "Shared Experiences Are Amplified," *Psychological Science* 25, no. 12 (2014): 2209–16.

CHAPTER 8

1. Richard McElroy and Catherine J. Smith, "The Impact of Clinic Design on Patient Anxiety in Dental Settings," *Journal of Dental Research* 92, no. 6 (2013): 510–15.
2. Li Lan and Zhiqiang Lian, "Use of Neurobehavioral Tests to Evaluate the Effects of Indoor Environment Quality on Productivity," *Building and Environment* 45, no. 5 (2010): 1268–77.
3. Jennifer A. Veitch and Guy R. Newsham, "Exercised Control, Lighting Choices, and Energy Use: An Office Simulation Experiment," *Journal of Environmental Psychology* 20, no. 3 (2000): 219–37.
4. Edward T. Hall, *The Hidden Dimension* (Garden City, NY: Doubleday, 1966).
5. Howard B. Beckman et al., "The Doctor-Patient Relationship and Malpractice," *Archives of Internal Medicine* 154, no. 12 (1994): 1365–70.
6. Paul S. Appelbaum, Charles W. Lidz, and Alan Meisel, *Informed Consent: Legal Theory and Clinical Practice* (New York: Oxford University Press, 1987).
7. Igor Knez, "Effects of Color of Light on Nonvisual Psychological Processes," *Journal of Environmental Psychology* 21, no. 2 (2001): 201–8.
8. Jacqueline C. Vischer, "Towards an Environmental Psychology of Workspace: How People Are Affected by Environments for Work," *Architectural Science Review* 51, no. 2 (2008): 97–108.

9. Judee K. Burgoon, "A Communication Model of Personal Space Violations: Explication and an Initial Test," *Human Communication Research* 4, no. 2 (1978): 129–42.
10. Penelope Brown and Stephen C. Levinson, *Politeness: Some Universals in Language Usage* (Cambridge: Cambridge University Press, 1987).
11. Paul Springer and Morton Deutsch, *Left Brain, Right Ear: Asymmetry in Auditory Processing* (New York: Academic Press, 1998).
12. Lena Sisco, *Honest Answers: Interview and Negotiation Skills to Get to the Truth* (Nashville: HarperCollins Leadership, 2024).
13. K. H. Teigen, "Yerkes-Dodson: A Law for All Seasons," *Theory & Psychology* 4, no. 4 (1994): 525–47.

CHAPTER 9

1. Beverly L. Brown, Howard Giles, and John N. Thakerar, "Preparation and Anxiety: Insights from the NFL and Secret Service," *Journal of Social Psychology* 125, no. 6 (1985): 669–73.
2. Fernand Gobet and Herbert A. Simon. "Expert Chess Memory: Revisiting the Chunking Hypothesis." *Memory* 6, no. 3 (1998): 225–55. https://doi.org/10.1080/741942359.
3. Robert P. Brown, "Lowering Anxiety Through Breathing Exercises," *Journal of Applied Psychology* 91, no. 4 (2006): 743–50.
4. Pablo Duran, Iris Tapiero, and Patrick Michael, "The Effects of Physical Fitness on Anxiety and Stress Levels," *Journal of Health Psychology* 23, no. 10 (2018): 1328–36.
5. Steven Johnson, *Where Good Ideas Come From: The Natural History of Innovation* (New York: Riverhead Books, 2010).
6. Ian M. James and Brian Savage, "The Use of Beta-Blockers in the Treatment of Performance Anxiety," *American Journal of Psychiatry* 141, no. 8 (1984): 1038–42.
7. Viktor E. Frankl, *Man's Search for Meaning* (Boston: Beacon Press, 1946).
8. Michael J. McMains and Wayman C. Mullins, *Crisis Negotiations: Managing Critical Incidents and Hostage Situations in Law Enforcement and Corrections*, 5th ed. (New York: Routledge, 2020).

CHAPTER 10

1. Ethan S. Bromberg-Martin, Masayuki Matsumoto, and Okihide Hikosaka, "Dopamine in Motivational Control: Rewarding, Aversive, and Alerting," *Frontiers in Behavioral Neuroscience* 3 (2009): 5.
2. John D. Salamone and Mercè Correa, "The Mysterious Motivational Functions of Mesolimbic Dopamine," *Neuron* 76, no. 3 (2012): 470–85.
3. Sally S. Dickerson and Margaret E. Kemeny, "Acute Stressors and Cortisol Responses: A Theoretical Integration and Synthesis of Laboratory Research," *Psychological Bulletin* 130, no. 3 (2004): 355–91.
4. Solomon E. Asch, "Effects of Group Pressure upon the Modification and Distortion of Judgments," In *Groups, Leadership and Men*, edited by Harold Guetzkow (Pittsburgh: Carnegie Press, 1951), 177–90.
5. Paul Ekman and Maureen O'Sullivan, "Who Can Catch a Liar?" *American Psychologist* 46, no. 9 (1991): 913–20.
6. Adrian F. Ward, Kristen Duke, Ayelet Gneezy, and Maarten W. Bos, "Brain Drain: The Mere Presence of One's Own Smartphone Reduces Available Cognitive Capacity," *Journal of the Association for Consumer Research* 2, no. 2 (2017): 140–54.
7. C. L. Kleinke, "Gaze and Eye Contact: A Research Review," *Psychological Bulletin* 100, no. 1 (1986): 78–100.
8. John Sweller, "Cognitive Load During Problem Solving: Effects on Learning," *Cognitive Science* 12, no. 2 (1988): 257–85.
9. Aldert Vrij, *Detecting Lies and Deceit: Pitfalls and Opportunities* (Chichester, UK: Wiley, 2008).
10. Abraham H. Maslow, "A Theory of Human Motivation," *Psychological Review* 50, no. 4 (1943): 370–96.
11. Jeffrey A. Hall, "How Many Hours Does It Take to Make a Friend?" *Journal of Social and Personal Relationships* 35, no. 2 (2018): 225–40.
12. Tony Alessandra, *The Platinum Rule: Discover the Four Basic Business Personalities and How They Can Lead You to Success* (New York: Warner Books, 1996).
13. Hanns Scharff, *Interrogation and Humanity: The Legacy of Hanns Scharff* (New York: Random House, 2003), 45–47.

14. Richard H. Thaler and Cass R. Sunstein, *Nudge: Improving Decisions About Health, Wealth, and Happiness* (New Haven, CT: Yale University Press, 2008).
15. Robert B Cialdini, *Influence: The Psychology of Persuasion* (New York: Harper Business, 2009).

CHAPTER 11

1. Stephen R. Covey, *The 7 Habits of Highly Effective People: Powerful Lessons in Personal Change* (New York: Free Press, 1989).
2. Carl R. Rogers and Richard E. Farson, "Active Listening," in *Communicating in Business Today*, eds. Ruth S. Matteson and Cynthia M. Baldwin (Boston: Houghton Mifflin, 1987), 54–64.
3. Daniel Goleman, *Emotional Intelligence: Why It Can Matter More Than IQ* (New York: Bantam Books, 1995).
4. Mark L. Knapp and John A. Daly, eds., *The SAGE Handbook of Interpersonal Communication*, 4th ed. (Thousand Oaks, CA: SAGE Publications, 2011).
5. Judee K. Burgoon, Laura K. Guerrero, and Valerie Manusov, *Nonverbal Communication*, 3rd ed. (Boston: Pearson, 2011).
6. T. L. Chartrand and J. A. Bargh, "The Chameleon Effect: The Perception–Behavior Link and Social Interaction," *Journal of Personality and Social Psychology* 76, no. 6 (1999): 893.
7. Abbie Jean Maroño, *The Role of Closeness in the Relationship Between Nonverbal Mimicry and Cooperation* (PhD diss., Lancaster University, 2022).
8. J. K. Burgoon, L. K. Guerrero, and V. Manusov, *Nonverbal Communication* (Pearson, 2011).
9. K. Patterson, J. Grenny, R. McMillan, and A. Switzler, *Crucial Conversations: Tools for Talking When Stakes Are High* (New York: McGraw-Hill, 2011).
10. D. Byrne, *The Attraction Paradigm* (Cambridge, MA: Academic Press, 1971).
11. Joe Navarro, *What Every Body Is Saying: An Ex-FBI Agent's Guide to Speed-Reading People* (New York: HarperCollins, 2008).

12. E. Hatfield, J. T. Cacioppo, and R. L. Rapson, *Emotional Contagion* (Cambridge: Cambridge University Press, 1994).
13. W. W. Maddux, E. Mullen, and A. D. Galinsky, "Chameleons Bake Bigger Pies and Take Bigger Pieces: Strategic Behavioral Mimicry Facilitates Negotiation Outcomes," *Journal of Experimental Social Psychology*, 44, no. 2 (2008): 461–68.

CHAPTER 12

1. Philip Houston, Michael Floyd, and Susan Carnicero, *Spy the Lie: Former CIA Officers Teach You How to Detect Deception* (New York: St. Martin's Press, 2012).
2. Tomasz Witkowski, "Thirty-Five Years of Research on Neuro-Linguistic Programming. NLP Research Data Base: State of the Art or Pseudoscientific Decoration?" *Polish Psychological Bulletin* 41, no. 2 (2010): 58–66.
3. Aldert Vrij, Samantha Mann, and Ronald P. Fisher, "Information-Gathering Interviews and the Detection of Deception," *Legal and Criminological Psychology* 11, no. 1 (2006): 159–76.
4. Joe Navarro, *What Every Body Is Saying: An Ex-FBI Agent's Guide to Speed-Reading People* (New York: William Morrow Paperbacks, 2008).
5. Thomas Gilovich, Victoria Husted Medvec, and Kenneth Savitsky, "The Spotlight Effect in Social Judgment: An Egocentric Bias in Estimates of the Salience of One's Own Actions and Appearance," *Journal of Personality and Social Psychology* 78, no. 2 (2000): 211–22.
6. Aldert Vrij, Sharon Leal, Pär Anders Granhag, Samantha Mann, Ronald P. Fisher, Ray Bull, and Anne-Maartje C. Zuur, "Increasing Cognitive Load to Facilitate Lie Detection: The Benefit of Recalling an Event in Reverse Order," *Law and Human Behavior* 32, no. 3 (2008): 253–65.
7. Leon Festinger, *A Theory of Cognitive Dissonance* (Stanford, CA: Stanford University Press, 1957).
8. B. M. DePaulo, et al., "Cues to Deception," *Psychological Bulletin* 129, no. 1 (2003): 74–118.
9. Saul M. Kassin, Christian A. Meissner, and Rebecca J. Norwick, "'I'd Know a False Confession If I Saw One': A Comparative Study of College Students and Police Investigators," *Law and Human Behavior* 29, no. 2 (2005): 211–27.

10. Robert W. Levenson, "Autonomic Nervous System Differences Among Emotions," *Psychological Science* 3, no. 1 (1992): 23–27, https://doi.org/10.1111/j.1467-9280.1992.tb00251.x.
11. David Matsumoto and Hyi Sung Hwang, "Reading Facial Expressions of Emotion," *Psychological Science* 22, no. 9 (2011): 1138–44, https://doi.org/10.1177/0956797611419705.
12. Paul Ekman, *Telling Lies: Clues to Deceit in the Marketplace, Politics, and Marriage*, 3rd ed. (New York: W. W. Norton & Company, 2009), 162–74.
13. Bella M. DePaulo et al., "Cues to Deception," *Psychological Bulletin* 129, no. 1 (2003): 74–118.
14. Aldert Vrij, *Detecting Lies and Deceit: Pitfalls and Opportunities*, 2nd ed. (Chichester, UK: Wiley, 2008), 157–59.
15. Bella M. DePaulo, James J. Lindsay, Brian E. Malone, Laura Muhlenbruck, Kelly Charlton, and Harris Cooper, "Cues to Deception," *Psychological Bulletin* 129, no. 1 (2003): 74–118.

CHAPTER 13

1. Fred E. Inbau and John E. Reid, *Criminal Interrogation and Confessions*, 5th ed. (Burlington, MA: Jones & Bartlett Learning), 2013.
2. Brian C. Jayne and Joseph P. Buckley, *The Investigator Anthology: A Compilation of Articles and Essays About the Reid Technique of Interviewing and Interrogation* (Chicago: John E. Reid & Associates, 2001).
3. Jack Schafer, *The Like Switch: An Ex-FBI Agent's Guide to Influencing, Attracting, and Winning People Over* (New York: Simon and Schuster, 2011).
4. Saul M. Kassin, Steven A. Drizin, Thomas Grisso, et al., *Police-Induced Confessions: Risk Factors and Recommendations, Law and Human Behavior* 34, no. 1 (2010): 3–38.
5. Gisli H. Gudjonsson, *The Psychology of Interrogations and Confessions: A Handbook* (Chichester, UK: Wiley, 2003).

CHAPTER 14

1. Sun Tzu, *The Art of War*, trans. Samuel B. Griffith (New York: Oxford University Press, 1963), 101.

2. Saul M. Kassin and Gisli H. Gudjonsson, "The Psychology of Confessions: A Review of the Literature and Issues," *Psychological Science in the Public Interest* 5, no. 2 (2004): 33–67.
3. Aldert Vrij, *Detecting Lies and Deceit: Pitfalls and Opportunities*, 2nd ed. (Chichester, England: Wiley, 2008).
4. Gisli H. Gudjonsson, *The Psychology of Interrogations and Confessions: A Handbook* (Chichester, England: Wiley, 2003).
5. Chip Heath and Dan Heath, *Made to Stick: Why Some Ideas Survive and Others Die* (New York: Random House, 2007), 243.
6. Melanie C. Green and Timothy C. Brock, "The Role of Transportation in the Persuasiveness of Public Narratives," *Journal of Personality and Social Psychology* 79, no. 5 (2000): 701–21.
7. Tom Van Laer, Ko de Ruyter, Luca M. Visconti, and Martin Wetzels, "The Extended Transportation-Imagery Model: A Meta-Analysis of the Antecedents and Consequences of Consumers' Narrative Transportation," *Journal of Consumer Research* 40, no. 5 (2014): 797–817.
8. Dedre Gentner, "Structure-Mapping: A Theoretical Framework for Analogy," *Cognitive Science* 7, no. 2 (1983): 155–70.
9. John E. Reid and Associates, *The Reid Technique of Interviewing and Interrogation*, 5th ed. (Chicago: John E. Reid and Associates, 2013), 291–95.

ABOUT THE AUTHOR

Brad Beeler recently retired after a distinguished 25-year career as a Special Agent with the United States Secret Service, where he became one of the agency's most respected polygraph examiners and communicators. His final assignment was as an instructor at the National Center for Credibility Assessment at Fort Jackson, South Carolina, where he trained thousands of federal agents, including professionals from the FBI, CIA, NSA, military intelligence, and law enforcement agencies across the country. His expertise in credibility assessment, deception detection, and elicitation techniques has significantly influenced the careers of those responsible for protecting national security and uncovering the truth during high-stakes interviews and interrogations.

Over the course of his career, Brad conducted more criminal polygraph examinations than any other Special Agent in Secret Service history. He has secured hundreds of confessions in high-profile investigations nationwide, particularly in cases involving child exploitation and homicide. In addition to his investigative work, Brad served on numerous protective assignments, ensuring the safety of US presidents and foreign dignitaries.

Recognized throughout federal law enforcement as an expert in communication and influence, Brad has delivered presentations across the United States and internationally to agencies seeking to enhance their ability to detect deception, improve interviewing techniques, and elicit truthful disclosures. He holds a master's degree in criminology and was honored as the US Secret Service Special Agent of the Year for his outstanding contributions to combating crimes against children. He resides in South Carolina with his wife of 26 years and their two children.

CONNECT WITH BRAD BEELER:

BradleyBeeler.com
LinkedIn: linkedin.com/in/bradbeeler1865
Instagram: @bradbeeler1865